PARENTING
PARTNERSHIPS

PARENTING PARTNERSHIPS

The Marriage-Free

Way to Have, Share,

and Prioritize

Your Child

FRANK
VEGA

PARENTING PARTNERSHIPS

THE MARRIAGE-FREE WAY TO HAVE, SHARE, AND PRIORITIZE YOUR CHILD

FRANK VEGA

Requests for permission to make copies of any part of the work should be emailed to the following address: frank@friendfamilylover.org
Published and distributed by Merack Publishing.

Library of Congress Control Number: 2022916613
Vega, Frank
Parenting Partnerships:
The Marriage-Free Way to Have, Share, and Prioritize Your Child

ISBN: Paperback 978-1-957048-70-3
eBook 978-1-957048-71-0
Hardcover 978-1-957048-72-7

DEDICATION

To my eldest Vega Boys and my Parenting Partners

CONTENTS

Preface   I

CHAPTER I
A New Dynamic Bringing Children Into the World   3

CHAPTER 2
Our Changing Attitudes Toward Marriage and Sex   19

CHAPTER 3
Parenting Partnerships: How's It Better,
Motivations to Pursue, and How Do We Consummate?   57

CHAPTER 4
My First Parenting Partnership   77

CHAPTER 5
Parenting Partnership Formation Basics   93

CHAPTER 6
Establishing Important Legal Documents   IOI

CHAPTER 7
Creating a Shared Expectations Document   123

CHAPTER 8
Things We Wish We'd Discussed or Done   I4I

CHAPTER 9
Anna's Experience   155

CHAPTER IO
Societal Reaction   173

CHAPTER 11
My Second Parenting Partnership   187

CHAPTER 12
Finding Love Post-Parenting Partnerships   199

CHAPTER 13
Natalie's Experience   205

CHAPTER 14
Fundamental and Important Interactions Within the Ecosystem   211

Conclusion   225

Acknowledgments   229

Endnotes   231

PREFACE

The personal events in this book began twenty years ago but the megatrends that made them necessary, possible and viable began decades and millenia before. The seismic changes around society's attitude concerning dating, marriage, conception, and child-rearing have hit the past couple of generations hard, and with an ever-quickening pace. Everything around courtship, personal opportunities and individualism is different from what our grandparents—and even our parents—experienced. There is a lot of negativity, confusion and frustration with the current state of "finding love." Starting with this book, we are wading into that space to share our story of dreams fulfilled, positive impacts on multiple lives, odds being crushed, traditions flaunted and what appears to be a happily-ever-after ending where four humans have set four newer humans positively on their own paths.

It's bittersweet that this book has taken five years to complete—way too long of an undertaking, but with every passing year a more confident, validated premise. The story I am honored to share on behalf of all the people I hold dearest in life is about instinct, desire and commitment to parenting trumping long-held societal norms and judgments. We'll share first-hand experiences from our two Parenting Partnerships. We have lived it. We *are* living it. We will be living it for the rest of our lives. You'll learn what Parenting Partnerships are like, how they work, and why we are proponents. Love for your child is pure, beautiful and infinite, what else in this human experience can make that claim?

While we live in a flawed modern society it still affords opportunities for some happiness as it evolves, for many that centers on family. Objectively, it's still the best time ever to be alive. More importantly, it's the only time we'll ever be on this planet so we must strive to live life to the fullest... and to me that meant becoming a father. It is our sincere wish that our efforts in writing this book can bring some direction, clarity, and joy to you and a few other hearts who yearn for children.

CHAPTER 1

A NEW DYNAMIC BRINGING CHILDREN INTO THE WORLD

There are essentially four different scenarios by which children come into the modern world:

1. Two people are married and conceive a child. They raise that child together for the duration of the marriage (until death or divorce).

2. Two people have a loosely defined romantic relationship where a pregnancy occurs. Choices ensue.

3. A woman becomes a single mother—either via planned or unplanned pregnancy.

4. Two adults with no future romantic intentions choose to pre-plan a pregnancy where both partners have committed to raising the child.

Scenarios 1 and 2 are well known to all and have been commonplace for the entirety of recorded human existence. Scenario 3 has also been a constant, but with significant broadening over the past eighty years due to changing societal norms and technological advancements, so it also qualifies as well known, but also evolving. People have been having babies for millenia in these three ways. But in modern societies, Scenario 4 has started to emerge as a viable option.

Large scale forces—economics, religion and societal norms—have demanded the coupling of marriage and child conception as a singular answer, often with inefficient and unhealthy results. People wanting children were pressured to subscribe to a certain set of beliefs, get married on a hurried timeline and contort themselves into a predefined box—or live with shame and stigma. Love and happiness were occasional byproducts, but ultimately not as important as outputting kids and following the prescribed rules. So, whether you wanted to marry or not, it was expected that a traditional marriage would accompany a pregnancy.

After centuries of playing by those rules, many people are questioning the very basis of traditional marriage for a variety of valid reasons and furthermore, the need for romantic love as a prerequisite for parenthood. The impetus for many of these questions stems from positive changes in modern society, specifically in large urban centers in the United States (U.S.) and some other parts of the world, which offer options that were not available to previous generations. There are now rules of law and a code of conduct that govern shared parenting responsibilities and custody. Our collective standard of living is significantly higher. Women have greater access to education and careers allowing for success on their own terms. Our lifespans are much longer, allowing people to procreate during a different life phase. Technology allows us to easily share financial resources and find all varieties of romantic connections.

These changes and the decay of older assumptions have led to the emergence of a new way for a child to enter the world: Scenario 4, Parenting Partnerships.

This book will provide you with our personal story of the power of Parenting Partnerships along with practical, helpful tips to possibly start your own Parenting Partnership journey.

WHAT IS A PARENTING PARTNERSHIP?

A Parenting Partnership is two adults committing to having and raising a child together without any romantic involvement. More precisely the key elements that define a Parenting Partnership are that both parents entered the relationship *willingly*, had a child together *deliberately*, and are both deeply *committed* to creating a healthy child-rearing environment without *any romantic commitment* between the two of them in the present or the future.

A Parenting Partnership should not be confused with other terms you may have heard in the media, the most popular of which is co-parenting; defined as, "a post-divorce parenting arrangement in which both parents continue to jointly participate in their children's upbringing and activities. This involves a substantial amount of interaction between the parents (both in public and in private)."[1] You've likely heard someone say, "We are co-parenting." And while they may be divorcées, they may not be. In today's parlance, the usage of co-parenting has been expanded beyond the above definition to encompass a multitude of parenting arrangements that are not your basic traditional marriage or divorced parents: never-married, parallel parenting, baby mama/baby daddy, communal living, multiple-parent scenarios, and blended families. In all of these arrangements unmarried parents work together to meet their children's needs: shared expenses, spending time together with the children at events or gatherings, important decision making, extended family interactions, even cohabitation.

So while similar, co-parenting is more of a catch all term that at best is a bland descriptor and at worse has a sterile, negative connotation due to its overwhelming association with divorced parents, unplanned pregnancies and Hollywood press releases. Co–parenting can be positive or can include high levels of bitterness and rancor. In many cases, co-parents seldom work well together as a team; they are adversaries in many ways. They reluctantly tolerate each other because they have to for their children, even though they may loathe doing so. The children sense this hostility and it can have many negative effects.

Parenting Partnership on the other hand is a very clear, positive identifier that provides a more precise categorization to quickly explain the origin and relationship we parents have to one another and our child. For these reasons and many others we rarely use co-parenting to describe our situation.

Two other terms that some people, and many academics, use to describe the exact same arrangement as "Parenting Partnership" are Platonic Parenting and Elective Co-Parenting. Between these three terms, we use the term "Parenting Partnership" because:

1. It's more accurate—it better speaks to the choices we made and the ongoing relationship between the two parents. The term partnerships denotes growth, longevity and stability with equal work effort through good times and bad. We "partner as parents" to raise our child. Saying we are "platonic" doesn't hold the same weight and isn't really accurate as we function in ways both higher and lower than friends would. Using the term "elective" sounds like we have a choice to participate or withdraw which is 100% inaccurate; this is not an educational course or an outpatient surgery.

2. It is easier to say and understand, "This is my Parenting Partner Frank." It works well as an introduction. Introducing someone as "My Elective Co-Parenting Partner" is less than eloquent and hearkens to the divorcee status of co-parenting. Stating this is my "Platonic Parent Frank" is awkward and doesn't even

make sense. Furthermore, introducing someone as a "Platonic Partner" can be confusing as there is a different movement whereby best friends are getting married which is called "Platonic Partnering" so this title doesn't distinguish the actual scenario.

Now that you are more familiar with what a Parenting Partnership *is*, let's also cover what a Parenting Partnership *is not*. It is not any of the following:

- Married parents

- A Good | Great | Awesome Marriage with kids, where two people are emotionally, physically, and financially bound to one another.

- An uninspiring marriage with kids where two people feel unfulfilled and "stay together for the kids" sometimes called a Parenting Marriage.[2]

- An unhealthy, toxic or abusive marriage with kids where the partners feel trapped or fear for their safety.

- Divorced parents

- A failed marriage with an amicable divorce resulting in co-parenting.

- A failed marriage with residual contempt and high-conflict resulting in parallel parenting (parenting with limited interactions and no shared goals).

- A long-term romantic relationship with a planned pregnancy

- Unwed people in a healthy romantic relationship who planned to have and raise a child together.

- A failed romantic relationship between two unwed people who had planned to have and raise a child together.

- The result of an unplanned pregnancy

- Unwed people in a healthy, romantic relationship who have a child by way of an unplanned pregnancy.

- A failed romantic relationship between two unwed people who have a child by way of an unplanned pregnancy.

- Any of the varieties of casual sex conception (often referred to as baby mama/baby daddy) resulting in single motherhood or single fatherhood where the other parent is reluctantly involved, not involved, or not known.

- Single parenthood through planned pregnancy

- A woman who planned to get pregnant and raise a child alone.

- A man who planned to conceive and raise a child alone via egg donor and/or surrogate.

So to reiterate, the key elements that define a Parenting Partnership are that both parents entered the relationship *willingly*, had a child together *deliberately*, they are both deeply *committed* to creating a healthy child-rearing environment without *any romantic commitment* between the two of them.

For these reasons and others, we use Parenting Partnership to describe our situation. If when using this term there is noticeable confusion, we quickly add, "we partner together to parent our child, but are not romantically involved." Quick, simple, colloquial and to the point. Accurately reflecting our past choices, present status and overall goal. We are two parents who work together in partnership towards raising a happy, healthy, and well-adjusted child.

EARLY ADOPTERS, NOT THE PIONEERS

At this point in the story, "we" encompasses myself and my first Parenting Partner Anna. The two of us first decided to enter into a Parenting Partnership in 2005 which put us at the forefront of this new dynamic, but not the absolute first to craft a Parenting Partnership. We didn't have a model to follow or anyone who could truly guide us. It was not mainstream then, so my Parenting Partner and I received a massive amount of feedback; questions, comments, and judgment.

However, these past seventeen years have really seen Parenting Partnerships gain ground in the public consciousness with many related articles appearing in a wide range of publications. These include a full feature in the New York Times in 2013 and mentions across all major media including: BBC.com, Parenting.com, *The Washington Post*, *The Guardian*, *The Telegraph*, and *Psychology Today*. NBC's *Today* show and other TV programs have run segments on the concept.

Multiple websites launched in the 2010s to offer guidance and services to adults who were interested in learning more about Parenting Partnership arrangements, even going as far as to offer a matchmaking service to help you find a compatible partner. Some examples are: modfamily.com, prideangel.com, pollentree.com, babygaga.com and coparents.com.

Lastly, books on the subject are difficult to find, but one of the earliest was published in 2014 by Rachel Hope called *Family By Choice: Platonic Partnered Parenting* which features even another naming convention for the same concept.

SEVENTEEN YEARS AND COUNTING

All this positive news coverage and attention in recent years confirms something I've known for almost two decades. This non-traditional form of conceiving and raising children not only works, but offers tremendous benefits for both parents and children. I certainly didn't invent the concept, but I've been living it since 2005 and am one of a handful of people on the planet who is in two successful Parenting Partnerships. I am seventeen and a half years into a Parenting Partnership with Anna, as our conversations began before our son Robert was born in 2006. And I am twelve and a half years into another Parenting Partnership with Sophia, with whom I share my second son Anthony, who was born in 2011.

Furthermore, I am proof positive that having a Parenting Partnership (or two) will not inhibit you from finding a stellar romantic partner. I met my wife Natalie in 2012 at age forty.

Natalie and I went on to get married in 2017 and have an additional two children; so that's four children, all boys, for me. This puts me in three very unique positions. First, I'm able to compare and contrast Parenting Partnerships with traditional marriage from a participant and parent perspective. Second, I'm in two Parenting Partnerships so I can speak with twice the experience and you know I must really deeply believe in the concept to have committed a second time. And third, I have a foot in both the traditional marriage-focused world and the current dating dynamic, since I started dating in the 1980s and finished dating in the 2010s. For the purposes of this book, we'll cover how each Parenting Partnership began, how each one is going now, and what we've learned along the way. As you read the book, you'll begin to understand the tremendous opportunity and advantages that Parenting Partnerships offer to both parents and children.

Having a single Parenting Partnership is very straightforward and highly achievable. While we share this story with you, you'll see that my personal story is fairly complex. Keep in mind that the vast majority of people will never attempt two Parenting Partnerships and then enter into a traditional marriage, not to mention have four children. I don't want that complexity to detract from the straightforward simplicity of two adults entering into a Parenting Partnership to have one child. What I hope you take away from our story is very simple: that Parenting Partnerships are truly a viable, marriage-free way to have, share and prioritize your child.

YOUR 'HOW TO' BOOK ON PARENTING PARTNERSHIPS

While straightforward and achievable, becoming a Parenting Partner is still a major reality-altering decision as you will become both a parent and a long-term partner at the same time! Additionally, beyond being a lifelong commitment for you, it's also the same huge step for your Parenting Partner and of course the child you two are bringing into the world. As with all big decisions in life, there are pros and cons, advantages and disadvantages that need to be considered. This book will help you understand Parenting Partnerships on all levels—physical, emotional, logistical, spiritual and financial. The benefit of this book is that we can offer something that news articles and college theses on the subject lack—the viewpoint of those with firsthand experience and true passion for the idea. Our stories will give you deep, personal, direct advice from almost two decades of hands-on, real-world partnering and parenting. It will help you make a more informed decision and provide important pointers should you decide to enter into a Parenting Partnership.

IMPORTANT NOTES

1. This is NOT a book on how to parent a child, which is extremely important information. I strongly suggest you read a few parenting books before you start your journey, there are literally thousands of books on that subject.

2. This book is written for single people, in their late twenties, thirties and early forties who are living in large, socially progressive cities, so some of these concepts are NOT as applicable in small towns, rural areas or other parts of the world.

3. If you know you NEVER want to have kids, then this book is obviously not for you, but please read on so you can support others.

4. Heartbreakingly, there are a multitude of DIFFICULT, NEGATIVE outcomes that can happen when conceiving children for both the parents and child, so make sure you keep all of those in mind as you develop your deep commitment to becoming a parent.

5. I am a huge fan of both Parenting Partnerships and healthy marriages. I am proud of both my alternative lifestyle and my traditional union. But, I abhor sub-optimal marriages for the inefficiency, pressures and miscalculations that lead to them and the damage they inflict.

6. If you're eager to become a parent but traditional marriage is not an option, or just not what you want, you're in the right place. In the coming chapters we'll share insights to help you understand how Parenting Partnerships work and why they work so well. We'll begin by looking at macrotrends that are changing attitudes towards marriage and sex in the United States and how they are fueling lower marriage participation rates, delayed marriage, childbirth outside of marriage,

and single parenthood. We'll then run two large comparisons: the first being, Parenting Partnerships versus the three other scenarios for bringing a child into the world and the second being, natural insemination versus other forms of conception. Next will be the story of my first Parenting Partnership so you can understand how we chose this path. Chapters 5, 6, 7 and 8 will outline basic foundational steps, "set the floor" with a discussion of a legal custody document, communicate "hopes and dreams" through a Shared Expectations Document and provide a "learn from our journey" list of tips to give you the best chance for success.

7. I'm all about providing value in this book. You're investing the time to read it, so I want to deliver maximum information and insight. While most of this book is written from my point of view, I know you're wondering what my Parenting Partners' experiences have been over the seventeen and a half years of interactions and what my wife's more recent experiences have been as well. Your curiosity is spot on and makes for compelling reading so we added those chapters!! The final portion of the book features an interview with Anna, reactions from friends and family, details of my second Parenting Partnership with Sophia and finally my wife Natalie's story in her own words. You will garner valuable insight by hearing from them where they reveal their thoughts, opinions, hesitations, and reflections. Please try your best to put yourself in the shoes of all four parents, the

kids and anticipate the reactions of your friends and family. Lastly, think of who would be your top three potential Parenting Partners?!?

As most parents will attest, having and raising children is one of the most beautiful, transformational, enriching, and fulfilling parts of the entire human experience. It's also very challenging at times, requiring patience, empathy and communication. I think anyone who is so inclined should become a parent. Unfortunately, in society there is an unnecessary—and even unhealthy—pressure to approach family planning in the traditional chronological steps: find someone who is "perfect" for you, start dating, fall in love, get engaged, get married, be newlyweds for a while, then get pregnant and raise a family. Society, religion and tradition try to tell us this is the *only* way it should be done.

That is unequivocally incorrect.

Anyone who says you have to follow a traditional path is living in the past. There is no reason two stable adults can't skip some of the steps and get to the best part—raising healthy, happy, well-adjusted children who will go out into the world and make it a better place.

In practicality, if you are in your teens, or twenties then Parenting Partnerships should probably not be your first choice for having children. If you are young and healthy, you should prioritize and actively try to manifest a loving relationship as the foundation for having a family. I also challenge you to ask yourself how deeply you want children. What's influencing your decision? A Parenting Partnership should be entered into with much forethought and when you are sure it is the right time for YOU and your PARTNER to have a child. It's best for those who truly, truly want to have and raise a child. You need to have exhausted other options (some of which will be discussed in this book) including romantic love, and have searched your soul to confirm this is the right choice for you, and then have made a deep, discerning effort to find a kind, loving and responsible person with whom to enter into a Parenting Partnership.

If you are committed to raising a child and feel that a Parenting Partnership is your best option, we congratulate you and wish you nothing but the best!!

My children, my Parenting Partners and I are living proof that Parenting Partnerships are a superior alternative to forcing a bad marriage, not ever having children if you desire them, or going it alone as a single parent. Thousands of other enlightened parents are joining the Parenting Partnership movement. It is becoming more common all the time, and I predict it will continue gaining momentum toward being considered fully mainstream.

So, don't let societal norms, family expectations, medical constraints, religious guilt, your age, pressure from friends, or anything else prevent you from experiencing one of life's greatest gifts: parenthood. If traditional marriage is not in the cards for you, please know that Parenting Partnership is a viable, proven way to fulfill your dream of being a successful parent and lead you to a higher level of existence. And possibly—like it did for me—to the romantic partner of your dreams!

It's a lot to think about, I know. But reading this book and considering Parenting Partnerships is worth it. Let's get started.

CHAPTER 2

OUR CHANGING ATTITUDES TOWARD MARRIAGE AND SEX

Humans have been having offspring for millions of years without being tied to a marital structure. Procreation was about the survival of the human race and positive instinct. Then urban society began and marriage was highly promoted. For a while, it seemed to work. It wasn't perfect, but it served a purpose. Along the way it became apparent (to some more than others) that the traditional hetero-marriage model certainly wasn't for everyone and needed improvement. It didn't often lead to happiness and, sadly, more often than not nowadays leads to personal misery.

Apart from marriage, humanity also has a complex relationships with sex. Over millenia the human relationship with sex, marriage and procreating has gone through a number of phases. The information age and a cell phone in almost every hand has helped to propagate familiarity with the extremes of the human experience around sex, marriage and procreation, for better or for worse. The world today is a smorgasborg of cultures that each have their unique view of sex, marriage and children. Books such as *Sapiens* by Yuval Noah Harari, and *Sex at Dawn* by Cacilda Jethá and Christopher Ryan help us understand the changes over the past tens of thousands of years. For modern times books such as *The New I Do* by Susan Pease Gadoua and Vicki Larson, and *Monogomish* by Alex and Kate Smith are resources that explore untraditional relationship agreements. Three megatrends to focus upon are the ever-lengthening human lifespan coupled with higher living standards and personal freedoms. The confluence of all of these factors has led to a very unique point in human history.

This chapter, and this book, are by no means intended to slander the idea of marriage. Marriage, when succeeding is a joyous experience. I am married and a huge fan of healthy marriages. But sadly, my premise (and the apparent reality to anyone paying attention) is that out of 100 marriages, 50% end up in divorce, another 25-30% are romantic failures that continue on as "just OK marriages" / "unhealthy marriages" / "abusive marriages" and only 20% of those 100 marriages achieve a truly healthy, positive marital outcome as a Good | Great | Awesome Marriage.

For some, hearing that marriages really have a 75-80% failure rate will be controversial. Now that the "information age" in all of its iterations has provided more insight into the underbelly of the institution of marriage, it is easy to understand the decline in marriage interest and participation. We'll provide a quick overview of the macrotrends which have cascaded to cause this decline in marriage, the correlated decline in the number of children born into traditional marriages, the subsequent rise in non-traditional parenting structures, the new trend of many individuals to not ever get married or have children and the recently reached tipping point where 50% of children are no longer raised in traditional marriages.

For all of our societal past, and still in many parts of the world now, society has put immense pressure on young people, especially women, to get married quickly for a variety of antiquated reasons: to meet religious imperatives, for arranged marriages, to get teens out of the house, to have grandchildren, to "be a real man" or "make an honest woman out of you", because it is "what we all did". For those who are not pressured in these ways, dating with the intention to find a marital partner is horribly inefficient, basically broken and certainly farcical. If you desire to have a child, Parenting Partnerships are a valid response that is undoubtedly a more positive alternative than forcing a bad marriage or single parenting. For all of human existence, people have been having children, yet we still can't seem to figure out the relationship part. So, what if we put a pause on the relationships and skipped ahead to childrearing?

MARRIAGE IS IN DECLINE, BUT PEOPLE STILL WANT TO HAVE CHILDREN

Marriage is in decline but people still want to have children. This is one of the principle tenets of this book, and it's a trend that has led to a growing interest in Parenting Partnerships. Marriage is less attractive for reasons we'll review later, but parenthood remains popular. A Pew Research study found that 52% of millennials surveyed considered being a good parent one of the most important things in life. But only 30% considered having a successful marriage to be important.[3] Clearly, younger people in America value becoming a parent (and doing it well) over getting married. This is a great example of present day mindsets that are decoupling marriage from child conception.

But first, let's explore the first half of that statement above, that marriage is in decline. A 2017 article by the Pew Research Foundation found, "Half of U.S. adults today are married, a share that has remained relatively stable in recent years but is down nine percentage points over the past quarter century and dramatically different from the peak of 72% in 1960, according to newly released census data."[4] In other words, marriage rates plummeted twenty-two percent in the last sixty years, which is an overall decline of 30%.

Marriage is even in decline for parents with children. According to a May 2018 article in *Psychology Today*, "One out of every four parents (25%) is unmarried, compared to just seven percent (7%) in 1968. There are now twenty-four million children living with a parent who is not married (compared to nine million in 1968). Percentage-wise, that's 32% now, compared to 13% then."[5] The decoupling of marriage from sex and pregnancy has been happening for the past fifty years in modern society.

With more education, more life experiences available to us and longer life spans, traditional, monogamous marriage doesn't seem as appealing or sustainable. Despite this, many people still consider marriage a prerequisite for having children. This is a problem because in much of the developed world, reproduction rates have fallen well below the 2.1 children per two adult population replacement rate.[6]

•	Sweden:	1.9	• Italy:	1.4
•	Holland:	1.8	• Germany:	1.4
•	United States:	1.6	• Japan	1.4
•	Spain:	1.4	• South Korea	0.9

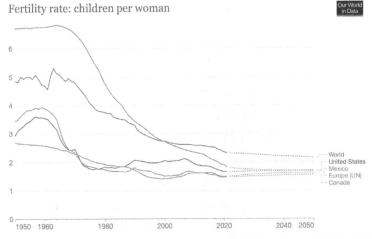

Fertility rate: children per woman

Source: United Nations - Population Division (2022)   OurWorldInData.org/future-population-growth • CC BY
Note: The total fertility rate is the number of children that would be born to a woman if she were to live to the end of her child-bearing years and give birth to children at the current age-specific fertility rates.

Specifically in the U.S., Kenneth Johnson, a demographer at the University of New Hampshire, has calculated that together with the rise in deaths—up by about 18% from 2019—the drop in births is contributing to the aging of the American population. A total of twenty-five states had more deaths than births last year, Dr. Johnson said, up from five states at the end of 2019.[7]

"The birth rate is the lowest it's ever been," he said. "At some point the question is going to be: The women who delayed having babies, are they ever going to have them? If they don't, that's a permanent notch in the American birth structure." New York Times, May 5, 2021.[8]

This has serious ramifications for our community, country, economy, culture and species. In regards to having more children, it would be beneficial to further lean into the notion of decoupling marriage from sex and procreation. It is my opinion that adults in our society need to become more familiar with other alternative parenting scenarios before a negative view of marriage completely wrecks the baby count.

While society historically pushed for heterosexual, monogamous marriage, there is no rule that requires parents to be in a romantic relationship. In fact (as I will argue later in this book), the passions and intense emotions that occur on the rollercoaster ride that almost all romantic relationships go through (especially as the participants age and mature over the years) does little to help children. Studies show it can actually harm them. A study done in 2019 lists withdrawal, acting out and emotional dysregulation as common behaviors displayed in children whose parents argue frequently.[9] Parental conflict is also a strong predictor of future depression and anxiety in children who live in unhappy homes. Brittany Wong's article *7 Ways You Can Damage Your Kids by Staying in a Bad Marriage* does an excellent job of outlining the damage unhappy marriages can have on the children involved.[10] Toxic marriages can affect a child's self-esteem and make them feel responsible for their parents' happiness. Parents are less present and are modeling an unhealthy relationship for their children.

Still, many people feel the pressure. *Why aren't you married yet? When are you going to propose? I want you to get married so I can have grandbabies.* It's difficult to break free from these ingrained expectations though it's happening slowly but surely. There are a multitude of books on the subject both broad and specific that are more exhaustive than what will be presented in this chapter should you desire further confirmation and edification.

Marriage in America has been losing popularity for many reasons. These include a fear of divorce and financial loss, increased longevity, the digital sexual revolution, a trend toward getting married later in life, prioritizing education, openness around LGBTQ+ and career expectations—along with the growing list of acceptable alternatives to marriage. Each of these reasons will resonate differently with each reader, but the mega trends are all pointing to the further decline of the number of people entering into traditional marriages. Let's take a closer look at these major reasons why marriage is in decline.

REASON #1

80% FAILURE RATE OF MARRIAGE

Fifty percent of marriages end in divorce.

We've all heard that statistic. But is it accurate? According to data collected by the Centers for Disease Control and Prevention, since the year 2000 the approximate annual divorce rate in the U.S. is right around 50%.[11] For example, in 2016 it was 46%, in 2010 and 2011 it was just under 53%, in 2008 it was 49%, and in 2012 it was almost exactly 50%. So, on average in the last twenty years, yes, we can say that roughly 50% of marriages end in divorce. Two caveats to this well worn factoid: 1) Second and third marriages have a higher rate of divorce than first time marriages which are estimated to have a 42% divorce rate[12] and 2) the numbers seem to indicate that Baby Boomers were much more divorce-prone (or marriage crazed?) than Gen X or Millennials who appear to be more picky and may over time drive down the divorce rate.[13] Dr. Larry Bumpass, an emeritus professor of sociology at the University of Wisconsin's Center for Demography and Ecology, has long held that divorce rates will eventually reach or exceed 50%. In an interview, he said that it was "probably right" that the official divorce statistics might fall below 50%, but that the rate would still be close. "About half is still a very sensible statement," he said.

But divorces are only the beginning of why 80% of marriages should be considered failures. Many marriages fail but they don't technically end in legal divorce. It's hard to say how many, as accurate data is difficult to obtain because it's unclear exactly what constitutes a failed marriage. We know divorce is a form of failure. But what about permanent separations? Or annulments? Or living under the same roof with limited interactions? Or sexless marriages? Or chronically unhealthy? Or marriages with constant infidelity? Or worse yet, manipulative, toxic, or abusive marriages? Everyone knows these marriages exist. If these figures were added in, then the number of failed marriages would climb much higher than 50%. Consider: projections for sexless marriages in the U.S. are between 15%-20% of couples[14] who report no sex in the last 12 months.

Now let's add in another category that constitutes marital failure against life aspirations, the large percentage of marriages where nothing is overtly wrong, but are uninspiring and unfulfilling. Just simply boring. These marriages don't end in abject failure, but they are certainly not what you, me, the participants or their friends and family would call successful. Millions of unhappily married couples begrudgingly stay together in dead-end marriages in a state of perpetual "Just OK" for all sorts of reasons: financial constraints, religious beliefs, habit, guilt, commitment, kids. How many times have you heard an unhappily married couple say, "I'm just staying to avoid the hassle." Or, "We'd get divorced but we can't afford it."[15] Or, "We're staying together for the children." While you have to admire their gumption for gutting it out, this certainly does not meet anyone's definition of a "successful marriage" and if you were told on your wedding day that it would be your fate, then I for one would turn tail and run from this type of "marriage failure".

DEBUNKING THE "STAY TOGETHER FOR THE KIDS" ARGUMENT

According to a 2017 article in *Psychology Today* titled "Why Bad Marriages Are Worse for Kids Than Divorce,"

"Kids forced to endure loveless marriages and to tolerate emotional tension day after day bear the full brunt of their parents' dysfunctional relationship. They intuitively feel their parents' unhappiness and sense their coldness and lack of intimacy. In many cases, children blame themselves, feeling their parents' combative relationship is somehow their fault. In such cases, staying together 'for the kids' is a cruel joke."[16]

In other words, the effect of a dysfunctional relationship between a child's feuding parents can have a significant impact on the child's well-being later in life. They may develop depression or anxiety, may trend towards unhealthy relationships, and experience trust issues or attachment issues.

So if you agree that an uninspiring marriage is a failure and add those to the litany of unhealthy marriages and the epidemic of divorces then an 80% marriage failure rate is valid for the participants, if not the statisticians. The exact percentage of failed marriages isn't as important as the undeniable fact that marriage is an extremely risk-laden commitment and well beyond the rote 50% divorce statistic. No matter how good the intentions of each spouse are when they enter the marriage, it is enormously difficult to sustain connection and happiness within this traditional confine. On a more positive note, while the premise is that only 20% of all attempted marriages end up as Good | Great | Awesome Marriages, that means that 40% of all presently married people are happily married which also feels right and matches up with anecdotal evidence.

What social scientists should be researching is whether married couples would choose to marry their partner again if they had a do over. Unfortunately, accurate data based on honest answers to the question, "How likely could you have found a better marital partner with whom you would have had a more complete marriage?" would be virtually impossible to collect not to mention heart-wrenching.

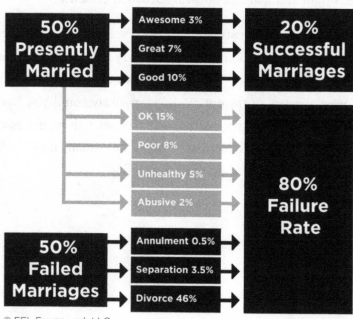

© FFL Framework LLC

As a result of so many marriages failing, many single adults look at the empirical and anecdotal data of friends and family member divorces and determine that the risk of marriage is just too great. For marriage to make sense today, there needs to be a significant increase in Good | Great | Awesome Marriage results. For me, and for many people, having success in marriage is found in properly answering the most important question of our human existence: *who will be my partner for life?* Followed in importance by: *will I have children?* Those two questions are the heart and soul of the next book I hope to write.

REASON #2
EXPERIENCING DIVORCE AND UNHAPPY MARRIAGES

When marriages end, they often end badly. Acrimony, lawyers, salacious allegations, pain, tears, embarrassment, loss of friends and social circles, and financial ruin. Yup, it's all in there. The end of a marriage can result in a steaming, toxic stew of regret seasoned with self-pity. When children are involved, you can add to that feelings of failure as a parent and guilt for the pain caused. I'm sure almost everyone reading this book has friends or family that are divorced and have seen the difficulties and devastation it creates.

First off, let's think about the emotional impact a failed marriage has on the adults involved. According to an article written in *Psychology Today*, divorced adults experience an increase in stress and depression, as well as a lower life satisfaction.[17] We can assume these struggles result from financial instability, trauma over custody battles, guilt and sadness over a failed relationship, and uncertainty about the future.

Children of divorced parents can experience an intense emotional impact as they observe sad and stressed parents learning to navigate a new family dynamic. When parents split up, children are often forced to move out of their home. Sometimes this requires them to change schools as well. Their whole world changes and this can threaten their sense of security and self. These children often harbor residual negative feelings toward marriage in general, leading them to avoid marriage in adulthood. In the Adverse Childhood Experiences survey, which is often used to assess the effects of trauma, parental separation and divorce is listed, as well as parental depression.[18] When parents split up, even if the separation is amicable, there are lasting effects on the children involved. Additionally, divorced parents likely want to prevent their adult children from experiencing divorce and thus downplay or caution against marriage, especially at earlier ages.

Consider that in a typical divorce, in addition to the emotional pain and turmoil that can last for years, there can be devastating financial costs. According to *businessinsider.com*, the average divorce in 2019 cost $15,000.[19] Paying for two lawyers can eat through a large portion of a married couple's savings. Then whatever is left over is split, usually fifty-fifty. In the end, after a contentious divorce each spouse may lose two-thirds of their total net worth—or all of it. In addition, after the divorce, couples still need to shell out money for court filings, mediation fees, and real estate fees if you need to sell a home. The financial cost of divorce can send some people into bankruptcy. Lastly, the two divorcées now need to reestablish themselves without the financial benefits of cohabitation so that they can care for themselves and their offspring.

Overall divorce is an awful experience so it is not surprising that many people fear the idea of being in a marriage that ends badly more than they value the benefits provided by a healthy marriage. It is a tough fact that in today's metropolitan societies almost everyone has experienced the negative impacts of divorce, and even more damning, that many more people have experienced mostly unhealthy, unhappy unions as opposed to healthy, fulfilling marriages.

REASON #3
CHANGING SOCIETAL STIGMAS AND PRESSURE

So many marriages ended in divorce over the past five decades in the U.S. that there is now significantly less social pressure to get married and little social stigma around being divorced. In the early 1900s divorce was a very difficult option to choose and, if enacted, was considered to be taboo. It was a source of shame for many people.

Starting in the 1970s, familiarity with divorce had permeated modern society and led to much less societal pressure to get married young and stay married if you were unhappy. Life choices that were once considered to be "alternative lifestyles" are becoming mainstream and accepted in the 2010s. Never getting married, living together but choosing not to marry, single parent households, or getting married much later in life are the new normal. According to a 2018 study published in the *Journal of Marriage and Family*, "…research on family changes has often invoked the decline in the 'normative imperative to marry' and the rise of the acceptability of alternative family forms as explanations… It is possible that the changing normative context played some role in the decline."[20]

For example, one formerly stigmatized alternative family structure in particular—single motherhood—is now considered commonplace. The number of children born outside of traditional marriage in the U.S. has hovered at about 40% for a number of years.[21] Not all single mothers find themselves in this position as the result of absentee partners. Some women choose to raise a child on their own. An organization called Single Mothers by Choice has more than thirty thousand members and is growing daily. According to the organization's website, "A Single Mother by Choice is someone who decides to become a mother, knowing that they will be the sole parent of their child – at least at the outset."[22]

Single motherhood has always existed. There have always been women who either by choice or circumstance have had babies on their own. What has changed is society's attitude and level of support for single mothers which has, in recent decades, become more accepting and accommodating—access to education, careers, laws, daycare infrastructure, working from home, flexible schedules, invention and prevalence of birth control—so this lessens their need to participate in a less-than optimal marriage.

Even more recently, there has been progress in most modern societies to support and destigmatize LGBTQ+ lifestyles whereby members of these communities no longer feel forced to participate in hetero-normative marriages as was the case for other LGBTQ+ individuals in the past.[23]

REASON #4
MARRIAGE WAS A NEED AND NOW IS A WANT

For thousands of years, religious and societal customs dictated you *needed* to get married. Rarely could someone become a high-functioning member of society without being in a marriage. In the past, women's inequality limited their ability to partake in career and life opportunities as they had little or no access to education, limited legal protections, and a lack of personal safety. As a woman, you simply felt you had to get married. Men also reaped the benefits of marriage. Gaining a wife got you children, a homemaker and access to sex. Nowadays, we look at those traditional male and female roles and think they sound archaic. They are antiquated in a multitude of ways, but both men, and especially women, have made amazing strides since then.

Even as society matured, there were huge economic benefits to getting married which helped to keep marriage as a "need". But these economic benefits of marriage, while still present, have diminished in importance with the ever rising 'Standard of Living' across the globe, specifically in North America and Northern Europe which have become extremely wealthy regions in the last two centuries. 'Standard of Living' is defined by Webster Dictionary as: the necessities, comforts, and luxuries enjoyed or aspired to by an individual or group. Please take the time to visit and enjoy one of my absolute favorite websites of all time, GapMinder.org. While there make sure to start with the all time classic *200 Years That Changed the World* video hosted by renowned Ted Talk speaker Hans Rosling (who sadly passed on in 2017). While it may not seem like it in today's media climate, this dramatic increase in 'Standard of Living' has given all of us in modern times significantly more flexibility in life choices than those that came before us. These megatends of longevity and wealth along with many other advantages of our modern world are expounded upon in great detail in the 2019 best seller *Fewer, Richer, Greener: Prospects for Humanity in the Age of Abundance* by Lawrence B. Siegel. Point being, there has never been a more abundant time to be alive and this affords modern society choices that past generations did not have.

Another driver of "need" was to avoid the aforementioned stigmas of not being married, women in the workplace, having children outside of marriage or being sexually outed. We now live in progressive societies where people of all sexes have the opportunity to have an education, a career, a household and access to family planning. This changes the whole dynamic of "needing" to get married. People have the option of choosing marriage because they want to, not because they need to. Today, most people get married because they truly believe their marriage will be successful, happy and healthy.

Not only did society highly *pressure* all to marry, provide *economic* incentives to marry, but it also made you feel the *need* by promoting an *idealization* of marriage having a positive outcome for everyone involved. From the 1950s through 1980s, media portrayed sanitized, perfect marital situations ala *Leave It to Beaver* to *The Cosby Show* that were not at all indicative of the average marriage. People got married and realized, "Oh that's not the way it really is", while sadly not often sharing those opinions openly. More recently, with information freely flowing, people are beginning to understand what the realities of marriage entail. Now that they better *understand*, feel *less pressured* and *don't need* to get married, they only partake if they truly want to.

We have left the era of needing to marry and have entered the era of wanting to marry, for better or for worse. And now that they have a choice, many people just don't want to get married!

REASON #5
CHANGING INDIVIDUAL PRIORITIES

Since marriage is no longer "needed" it follows that it's no longer the all-consuming goal for adults in this country as it once was—especially not for people in their teens, twenties and thirties. Instead of getting engaged young and planning a wedding, many single adults in their twenties and thirties are prioritizing education, career, and experiences.

Without the pressure to have children, many adults are choosing to skip marriage and kids altogether. According to a

2021 study done by The Pew Research Center, 44% of adults who do not have children state that it's very unlikely that they will become parents in the future.[24] Reasons range from medical issues, to financial concerns, to concerns about the state of the world. With almost half of grown adults expressing massive hesitation about parenting, it's no wonder marriage rates are on the decline.

Today, it is somewhat common and accepted to hear of individuals eschewing marriage and kids for career pursuits, hobbies, travel, absence of responsibilities or serial monogamy. Also more common is individuals expressing that they have "no religious affiliation", specifically Christian based Protestantism and Catholicism which are both very pro-marriage and pro-children in message

In U.S., roughly three-in-ten adults now religiously unaffiliated

% of U.S. adults who identify with ...

63% Christianity

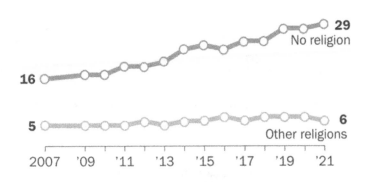

29 No religion

6 Other religions

2007   '09   '11   '13   '15   '17   '19   '21

Note: Those who did not answer are not shown.
Source: Data from 2020-21 based on Pew Research Center's National Public Opinion Reference Surveys (NPORS), conducted online and by mail among a nationally representative group of respondents recruited using address-based sampling. All data from 2019 and earlier from the Center's random-digit-dial telephone surveys, including the 2007 and 2014 Religious Landscape Studies. See Methodology for details.
"About Three-in-Ten U.S. Adults Are Now Religiously Unaffiliated"

PEW RESEARCH CENTER

Women's priorities have experienced an enormous transformation in the last fifty years. Up until the 1960s, most women did not go to college and many never entered the workforce. The most socially accepted option for young women was to get married and raise a family. Women are graduating from college, earning advanced degrees, entering the workforce, succeeding in careers and starting businesses in greater numbers than ever before with women making up 59.5% of college graduates in 2021, an all-time high in the United States.[25] These education and career related choices are delaying marriage for many and have made it completely unnecessary for others. Today, being a married, stay at home mom is the exception, not the rule.

REASON #6
THE SEXUAL DIGITAL REVOLUTION

Another motivation for marriage was consistent access to sex from a spouse. Up until the 1960s in the United States, religious and societal pressure discouraged sex outside of marriage. This is still the case in many corners of the U.S. and the world. How many high school sweethearts got married so they could have guiltless sex as often as they wanted? Waiting for marriage to lose one's virginity may have been reasonable if you were getting married in your teens and early twenties, but is unreasonable if you're getting married in your thirties. There is significantly less, to none whatsoever, stigma around premarital sex in today's modern society. Unwed, sexually active couples are common. Not only that, but getting consistent, reliable sexual fulfillment today doesn't actually require a relationship at all.

Before the internet, the pool of potential dating and sexual partners was limited. A single man or woman only had access to potential mates through a small number of channels: work, social activities, religious activities or their neighborhood. At best, the number of potential sexual partners or mates in the appropriate age range for the average person was a few hundred. Further reducing an individual's dating pool were strict societal and familial boundaries based upon religious, socioeconomic, sexual-preference, racial or ethnic filters.

Online dating exponentially expanded the number of potential sex partners one could meet. Now almost anyone, anywhere is a potential hookup. Urban living and the internet boosted potential sexual partners from a few hundred people to many tens of thousands. And for anyone willing to date long distance or virtually, the number of potential sexual partners is in the millions. Not to mention sexual release through pornography, online sex options and the loosening attitudes towards pay-for-play arrangements and sex workers.

Furthermore, the popularity and mainstream acceptance of mobile dating apps like Tinder, Bumble, and Hinge have helped to spawn and normalize a sex-positive, accessible dating culture. It's socially normal for adult men and women to meet their sexual needs by swiping right on their smartphone, with a potential sex partner showing up an hour later. Single people can have physical relationships easier than ever before. As a result, the notion of getting married to ensure consistent sex seems quaint, if not downright anachronistic.

This sexual freedom comes with reverberations in many forms. Some interesting points to note:

1. The aforementioned rise in pregnancies outside of marriage.

2. Sexually transmitted infections which had been significantly down ten years ago, surged in 2022 post-pandemic United States.[26]

3. After you have had more than one sexual partner before marriage your divorce rate in the first five years jumps significantly but doesn't continue to climb appreciably.[27]

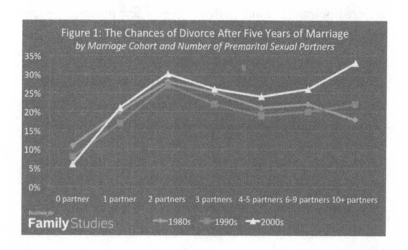

Figure 1: The Chances of Divorce After Five Years of Marriage by Marriage Cohort and Number of Premarital Sexual Partners

REASON #7
CHANGING TRENDS IN LIFE EXPECTANCY

People today live longer than they did in the last century and with a higher quality of life. Modern medicine, pharmaceuticals, advanced diagnostics, nutrition, exercise and science have lengthened the average life expectancy to eighty years in North America. If major advances in genetics, computational biology, epigenetics, gene sequencing, microarray technology, and human genome science continue at their current pace, some experts predict life expectancies will climb to 100 or even 200 years. At the same time, the child-bearing window has not changed markedly.

Historical and Projected Life Expectancy for the Total U.S. Population at Birth: 1960-2060

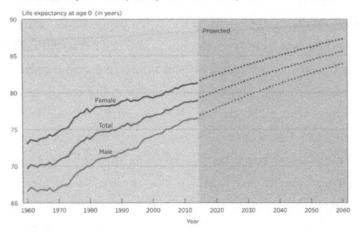

Sources: U.S. Census Bureau, 2017 National Population Projections, 2015-2060, and National Center for Health Statistics Life Tables, 1960-2014. <www.cdc.gov/nchs/data/nvsr/nvsr68/nvsr68_07-508.pdf>.

The average life expectancy in the mid 1800's was approximately forty years old, in 1900 it was forty-eight and in 1960 it was right at seventy. In 2019 depending on the study it reached eighty years and was still growing.[28] The Covid-19 pandemic, combined with tragedy of opioid and fentanyl overdoses in 2020 and 2021, caused the first retraction in decades losing one and a half years, with most projections assuming this loss to be rectified in 2023. So for tens of thousands of years until the 1800s it made sense that getting married young and having children young was an all-consuming goal for most people. This has only changed significantly in the past fifty years in some societies.

How will these advances affect marriage? Well, consider this— if in the near future medical breakthroughs increase expected lifespan in developed countries to 120 years, and you get married in your twenties, what are the odds that the marriage will last eighty or ninety years? People can change a lot in ten years let alone eighty years. If life expectancies really do lengthen significantly in the future, I believe this will further contribute to marriage's downward slide. In previous centuries when the average lifespan of a human was forty years, getting married young and having children quickly not only made sense, but was necessary. But as we enter the era of lifespans nearing ninety years, people are going to think twice about marriage. At the very least, I think they'll postpone marriage until much later in life (we cover this next in Reason #8). That said, they'll still want kids when young and will be having plenty of sex, which will further disassociate marriage, sex and conception.

As lifespans continue to increase, the trajectory of life experience also changes. An article published by the BBC describes this phenomenon, quoting what social scientists have termed, "Life History Theory."[29] In tougher historical times (i.e. during a World War or the Great Depression), teenagers were forced to grow up fast—getting jobs at a young age, marrying and reproducing during their late adolescent years and focusing on basic needs. Today, with life being more forgiving, teenagers are having a delayed transition into adulthood.

The article goes on to describe other cultural changes that have been sparked by longer lifespans, quoting Lynda Gratton and Andrew J. Scott, authors of *The 100-Year Life*.

"Greater longevity will soon begin to make the "three-stage" life of school, work and retirement feel outdated. One difference we should consider is the assumption that in our twenties we are meant to go immediately from schooling to a career. In the 100-year life we should consider taking a period of our twenties and dedicating ourselves to a new stage, exploration... Your decisions early in life impact the entirety of the rest of it... so it is rather absurd that we expect people in their late teens and early twenties to make decisions like what direction they want their lives to take. Instead they should have a period of exploring the world and trying different paths."

It goes without saying that, if adolescents are taking longer to mature, partly due to the fact that the human brain doesn't reach full development until twenty-five years of age,[30] and young adults are dedicating their twenties and thirties to exploration and life experience, the average age people choose to get married is also being delayed. Because, why would a rational person make multiple life-altering decisions before gaining some knowledge, insight and self-awareness?

REASON #8
DELAYING MARRIAGE = FEWER MARRIAGES AND CHILDREN

While the word "delaying" doesn't sound problematic, it may be. Because some portion of individuals who delay will ultimately not get married and/or have a child at all. The U.S. Census Bureau reported that in 2021 the average age of first marriage for women was 28.6 years and for men it was 30.4 years. That's the longest Americans have ever waited to get married. The graph below from the U.S. Census shows the progression.

Figure MS-2
Median age at first marriage: 1890 to present

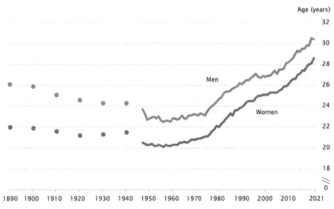

Source: U.S. Census Bureau, Decennial Censuses, 1890 to 1940, and Current Population Survey, Annual Social and Economic Supplements, 1947 to 2021.
Note: Starting in 2019, estimates for marriages now include same-sex married couples.

The correlated result of delaying marriage is that women are on average having children much later in life than ever before, but that is not the whole story. During their delay some women decide they don't want marriage at all, run out of time to partner before their reproductive years are over, decide they no longer want children, decide to have fewer children than they may have had if they had married at a younger age, or experience reproductive medical issues. For men three of these five reasons are also applicable. A 2018 article titled "As births decline in young women, they keep rising in forty-somethings. Here's why." appeared in *USA Today*.[31] It stated, "The United States is in the midst of a baby bust as birth rates fall in every age group of women except for one: women in their forties, according to government statistics released this week. While most babies are born to women in their twenties and thirties, the continued rise of older moms reflects a long-term shift to delayed childbearing."

Psychologists attribute the trend in women having children later to the same factors which were discussed in "Reason #5 - Changing Individual Priorities." According to the *USA Today* article, "Many women in their twenties and thirties are completing education and starting careers. They feel unready, financially and otherwise, to have babies," and, "Some women wait a long time to find the right person to have a baby with... By forty, they may go ahead with or without that perfect partner."

While the over forty group are having more kids than ever before, it's still a small amount of babies in the aggregate. Tragically for some, the serious issue of infertility occurs. This can happen naturally, but with sexually transmitted infections (STI's) on a dramatic rise, it is estimated that, "at least 20,000 women are rendered infertile by untreated STI's in the U.S. each year." New York Times May 17, 2022.[32]

REASON #9
MARRYING JUST FOR CHILDREN

Marrying just for children was a legitimate motivation for marriage in the past when life was short and children were needed. While marrying "just for children" is likely a suspect strategy for optimal marital happiness for a multitude of reasons, some would argue it may lead to more marital happiness due to reduced marital expectations that are met when the child arrives. In my mind it is analogous to getting married for money, status or attractiveness—all risky strategies when trying to achieve marital happiness.

Per religious and social structures, it was expected that every married couple would procreate with some religions having this as a core tenet similar to Christianity's: "be fruitful and multiply and fill the earth and subdue it." While having children very young is still a goal for some people, this is certainly less popular and for good reason. Children having children is not likely to lead to a positive marital outcome.

Still, it's not unheard of for adults to push for "marrying just for children." People still seek marriage with the primary agenda of having children, usually on a timeline, not because they are deeply in love with their partner. Have you ever heard this conversation? *I'm thirty-three with a good job and ready to have kids. My girlfriend has been around for a while so I am just gonna pop the question and make it happen. / I'm twenty-seven, closing in on twenty-eight, and my boyfriend is a really nice guy. I'm not super in love with him, but I think he'd be a good father. I really don't want to go back into the dating pool and I want a baby before I am thirty, so we need to get married.*

Two additional factors may be further inhibiting the "get married for the kids" strategy. First, that it is now well publicized how expensive children have become which many young people cite as an impediment to starting a family and second that many young people have negative outlooks on the future of the planet and human race which dissuades them from wanting to bring a child onto this planet.

If you do agree with Reason #9 you are not alone, as 'Mr. Wonderful' Kevin O'Leary of *Shark Tank* and author of *Cold Hard Truth On Men, Women and Money* that "the only reason you should marry is if you are planning to have children."[33]

When one or both partners decide to get married primarily to have a child, once they get what they really want out of the relationship, the marriage may become expendable. There is no longer a driving force behind participating in the marriage, and this has morbidly spawned a tongue-in-cheek descriptor of 'Praying Mantis Syndrome' where the partner who only wanted to procreate, once a parent, has no future use for the other partner. While not proven, this might help to explain some portion of the discrepancy whereby 80% of divorces are filed by women.[34]

REASON #10
UNREASONABLE ROMANTIC EXPECTATIONS

Even if a couple does choose to marry, going into the commitment with hope, realism and the best intentions, marriages can still fail. Many times, this is due to unrealistic romantic expectations. You can't expect your partner to be your perfect everything. They can't fulfill all of your needs. Maybe in the past with lower expectations of life and when surrounded by family and lifelong friends individuals did not require as much from their partners.

Psychologist Esther Perel wrote the following in an article called, "Why Modern Love is So Damn Hard"[35]:

Is it any wonder that, tied up in relying on a partner for compassion, reassurance, sexual excitement, financial partnership, etc. that we end up looking to them for identity or, even worse, for self-worth?

Combine that with the commodification of love, the increasingly omnipresent "is there somebody better?", and we have a recipe for decreasing the perceived "cost" of love. All the while increasing our expectations on our partnerships, and even adding more to the list, without really understanding what we're asking. This litany of expectations is a grand setup for failure. Once we strayed because marriage was not supposed to deliver love and passion. Today we stray because marriage fails to deliver the love, passion, and undivided attention it promised.

If you are looking to have all of your needs met by a single person, you are both being set up for failure. I'm squarely in the camp of "you need to be happy with yourself first." There are thousands of books on this topic and it's outside of the scope of this book. But the general consensus seems to be, if you don't like your own life and your own company, be careful expecting someone else to fulfill you.

Just in case this non-exhaustive list of ten reasons marriage is in decline isn't convincing enough for you or others, here's is an additional data point from the twenty-first century that provides a vivid "hindsight is 20/20" epiphany about how marriages during the idealized good ol' days of the 1950s-1990s were less than perfect:

GENETIC SURPRISES ARE PROOF THAT NOT ALL 1950s MARRIAGES WERE GREAT.

People often romanticize the past and with it the sanctity of marriage. We idolize great grandma and grandpa as icons of morality. We congratulate people who've made it to their fiftieth wedding anniversary and hold them up as a model of loving and committed relationships. The problem is, now that we have the technology to look into genetics, we have found many surprises. We can look two, three generations back and realize there was some serious "stepping out" occurring. Not everyone thought to be family are actually genetically related and fully a part of the family's bloodline.

While many people use genetic websites such as ancestry.com and 23andMe.com to find out their genealogy or ethnic origins, occasionally someone is blindsided by discovering that a) they do not share any DNA with their father, b) they have biological half brothers and sisters they never knew about, or c) that other family members are not paternally related to their families. In fact, a 2021 article published in a medical journal suggests that up to 10% of pregnancies have false paternity, while other sources declare the number is closer to 3%.[36]

This begs the question—if a marriage had non-paternal children born within the traditional constructs of marriage, was it a healthy, happy, honest union? This statistic goes to reinforce everything we've discussed thus far about the limitations of pressuring two people into marriage and furthers the hypothesis that marriage hasn't been working for many people for many generations.

THE DECLINE OF TRADITIONAL MARRIAGE WILL CONTINUE

Marriage is in serious decline both in numbers and in perception. The synergistic effects of the megatrends and changes we mentioned in Reasons 1 – 10 have brought on a new dating, marriage and child-conception dynamic in the major cities across North America, Europe and the world. Along the way to this new dynamic, multiple Malcolm Gladwell-esque tipping points have been hit:

- Young adults now believe career fulfillment more important than marital fulfillment[37]

- Young adults now cohabitate more than being married[38]

- More than 50% of children are raised outside of traditional family structure[39]

- 40.5% of all births were to unmarried women in 2020[40]

Americans more likely to say career enjoyment key to a fulfilling life than marriage

% saying each of the following is ____ for a man/woman to live a fulfilling life

■ Essential ■ Important, but ▨ Not important
not essential

Being married

For a man	16	54	29
For a woman	17	54	28

Being in a committed romantic relationship

For a man	26	59	14
For a woman	30	57	13

Other items:

Having a job or career they enjoy

For a man	57	39	3
For a woman	46	48	5

Having a lot of money

For a man	20	65	14
For a woman	15	68	16

Having children

For a man	16	58	25
For a woman	22	57	21

Note: Share of respondents who didn't offer an answer not shown. "Being in a committed romantic relationship" and "Being married" were each asked of a random half of the sample.
Source: Survey of U.S. adults conducted June 25-July 8, 2019.

PEW RESEARCH CENTER

Nonmarital childbearing has increased dramatically for women of all education levels

Percent of births occurring to unmarried women age 18+ by education, 1990 and 2016

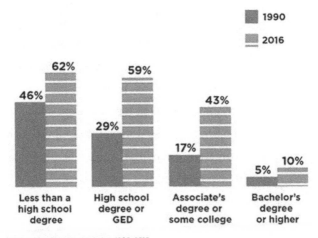

- ■ 1990
- ▦ 2016

Less than a high school degree: 46% / 62%
High school degree or GED: 29% / 59%
Associate's degree or some college: 17% / 43%
Bachelor's degree or higher: 5% / 10%

Source: Vital Statistics birth data 1990, 2016

Whether you find this to be positive or negative, it is the reality. Furthermore, these trends will likely continue and not reverse. For all the reasons above, in U.S. culture, people of child-bearing age are significantly less enchanted with the prospect of marriage than their parents and grandparents were. The decades-old notion that marriage is the one socially acceptable destiny for every adult who wants children has been pierced and deflated. Societal, economic and religious pressures to get married have abated.

Our modern society offers more paths to find fulfillment than just marriage and kids. Singles can dive in and out of the dating pool with a few taps on a smartphone to try to meet emotional and physical needs. This has made dating in this new age very difficult, with some individuals having a "no marriage" mindset and others not prioritizing seeking a marriage above education, career and/or experiences.

Navigating these changing dynamics should not prohibit responsible adults from having the joy of parenthood. Instead of marriage being a primary goal for everyone, many in society today tend to view marriage and having children as two distinct concepts to be pursued independently at an individual's own discretion, unencumbered by tradition or custom. It is no surprise, then, that a significant portion of unmarried adults are considering alternatives to traditional marriage such as Parenting Partnerships.

CHAPTER 3

PARENTING PARTNERSHIPS:
HOW'S IT BETTER, MOTIVATIONS TO PURSUE, AND HOW DO WE CONSUMMATE?

We've established that there's a huge change in attitudes toward marriage. The catch is, even with marriage in decline, people still really want to have children. As marriage and conception continue to decouple, Parenting Partnerships will be a growing part of that exploration and could even become the next logical progression in a post-marriage society.

Almost every parent will tell you that their greatest joy or accomplishment is their children and everything else pales in comparison. If raising children is a noble, worthwhile endeavor for many, but marriage is deemed too risky and likely to end badly for the majority of couples, it begs the question: Can we realistically decouple having well-adjusted children from the concept of marriage? I believe the answer is a resounding yes. Having and raising children provides such great joy and fulfillment it should not be denied to anyone just because they aren't married or don't want to be.

And with all the changes mentioned in Chapter Two, there have been, are, and will continue to be millions of people having children without being married: sperm donation, egg donation and single motherhood (both planned and unplanned) are all routes to having children without a marriage or a partner. Each of these options comes with significant upside, challenges and risks.

In this chapter, we'll be making the case that Parenting Partnerships offer many advantages for both the parent and child when compared to these single-parent options. In fact, in the following pages I'll make the case that for people with an aversion to marriage, Parenting Partnerships are the absolute best option for having kids. For those people that did desire marriage, but were not able to achieve a Good | Great | Awesome Marriage on their timeline, Parenting Partnerships are often a superior option to all other forms of unwed parenthood when you factor in both the parent and child. Let's start with the concept that ideologically has the most in common with Parenting Partnerships: choosing to become a single mother through a planned pregnancy.

PARENTING PARTNERSHIPS/PLANNED SINGLE MOTHERHOOD

Parenting Partnership closely aligns with single motherhood by choice, with the major similarities being that both are based on a planned pregnancy with much forethought and no expectations of a romantic connection. Both scenarios allow for the parent to find a romantic partner at a later date, or skip it completely. The true difference is a Parenting Partnership adds a second committed parent which, if all parties are their best selves, brings significant benefits for both the mother and child. For the mother these benefits include shared child-rearing responsibilities, additional extended family childcare options, extra contributed financial resources, and likely some amount of emotional support. Essentially, a mother would not be going it alone, but would have a deeply committed Parenting Partner whose help would allow her more personal freedom while having the baby less than 100% of the time, which in our experience can be a welcome break. This support can be very helpful for her mentally, physically and emotionally, plus this flexibility can help her to meet her own personal and career goals. Two parents can provide twice the resources, love and attention, decision-making capability, support system, safety net when things go wrong, and doubly reduce some risks. Additionally, the child now has two extended families providing that much more love, care, learning and safety net.

Sadly, it is well documented that children in single-parent homes face tougher odds on a number of important metrics as opposed to the reams of research which shows that children who are raised in a two parent home have, "stronger cognitive and motor skills, enjoy elevated levels of physical and mental health, become better problem-solvers, and are more confident, curious, and empathetic. They also show greater moral sensitivity and self-control."[41]

PARENTING PARTNERSHIPS/UNPLANNED SINGLE MOTHERHOOD

There are a multitude of ways a woman can find herself on the path to unplanned single motherhood. Some are dark and evil, scourge-of-our-society level occurrences. For most it is an unplanned pregnancy with a sexual partner of as little as one night or as long as many years. Unplanned pregnancies are a shock no matter what age or situation, but for unwed women it can disrupt her life arc by setting back education, career or life aspirations and opportunities. An order of magnitude lower, it is also a shock for the impregnating male, who may not have wanted to become a father. In some instances the two may be able to come to a healthy equilibrium, but often there is a rush of emotions that manifest themselves in some very negative ways as the two try to grapple with this unexpected situation. With love and dedication all things can work out for parents and child, but certainly a Parenting Partnership would be a positive alternative to any of the iterations of unplanned single motherhood.

PARENTING PARTNERSHIPS/DIVORCES

Parenting Partnerships are superior to "divorced with kids." This is fairly straightforward as divorce has a slew of negative experiences and attributes for the adults and children involved. While "things may have been learned" through the relationship and the divorce can even be amicable, it is still a hugely negative disruption for adults and offspring. The transition period from one dual-parent to two single-parent households can be very difficult and making custody arrangements work on top of all the other logistical changes is hard. Beyond child support payments, a spouse may also have to make significant alimony payments in divorce situations. An argument for divorces is that "the kids were brought into the world in a marriage" and there would be additional hours with the child prior to splitting up. All in all, the divorcees could have skipped the whole failed marriage and/or child together or have chosen to enter into a Parenting Partnership where they would still have had a child without the mess of a failed romance.

PARENTING PARTNERSHIPS/UNINSPIRING AND UNHEALTHY MARRIAGES

As for those who remain in sub-optimal marriages, Parenting Partnerships are certainly better than any abusive, toxic or unhealthy marriages as those are miserable for the parents and difficult, to severely negative, for the kids.

Parenting Partnerships start with the kids first, not ending up there after a romance dies/fades away. The child is not a byproduct of a relationship. The two parents didn't come together out of lust or desire or dreams of happily ever after that were later dashed in bitter disappointment. There is no lingering legacy of hurt feelings, jealousy, callousness or resentment. Rather, in Parenting Partnerships the two parents started with and always have had a lifelong shared goal—the best interest of their child. While all three of these scenarios allow for shared resources, teamwork and extended families to provide for their child, the economic benefits of living under one roof do not outweigh the restrictions on personal freedom and happiness. These unhappy marriages with children can pivot to being solely child-centric, but the marriage participants are still bound to each other in a multitude of restrictive ways along with the fact that kids generally see right through the charade. One of the major objections often levied against Parenting Partnerships is that the children don't see romantic love modeled between the parents. I would put forth that kids don't see it in these situations either, so in these instances and the single motherhood scenarios it is a non-factor.

It is a matter of opinion as to whether a Parenting Partnership is superior to an uninspiring, but not dysfunctional marriage. Stability of home for the child, everyday interaction between parents and child and the economic benefits of a shared household are the positives for the mediocre marriage versus the personal freedoms and potential for romantic happiness available to the parents within a Parenting Partnerships.

PARENTING PARTNERSHIPS/HAPPY COUPLES

Truly happy couples in a stable, healthy, Good | Great | Awesome Marriage or unwed relationship, that have a child and stay together for the long-term would very likely be a better situation for the partner and child than a Parenting Partnership. Having someone with whom to share life, snuggle at night and build a solid home is fantastic. Seeing your children every day is a joy. To reiterate, we are healthy marriage positive in all ways.

MOTIVATIONS FOR SEEKING A PARENTING PARTNERSHIP

Now that you have an idea of what constitutes a Parenting Partnership and the advantages of Parenting Partnerships over multiple other outcomes, let's look at the motivations for why someone would seek out a Parenting Partner with whom to have their child.

AVERSION TO MARRIAGE

For all the reasons outlined in Chapter Two, and many others, some people are dead set against marriage, but deeply want to be a parent. A Parenting Partnership might be the best option for them. Other excellent options would be adoption or establishing a long-term romantic relationship where both partners are committed to raising a child and not ever getting married (and hopefully not breaking up).

BEATING THE BIOLOGICAL CLOCK

The old bugaboo. This is a well documented and looming negative mile marker that has been portrayed constantly in media and the arts for the past fifty years. One of the factors driving the growing popularity of Parenting Partnerships is what is commonly called the biological clock. It's becoming more and more common for accomplished, educated, financially stable women (and to a lesser degree men), who have both the desire and potential to be wonderful parents, to find themselves running up against the same biological clocks that have existed for millenia: conceiving, being a youthful parent and seeing their grandchildren.

A century ago, the average age for women to be married was twenty-one years old. Generally, the couple was pregnant soon after. In that scenario, there are few concerns about a young woman's ability to reproduce. Medically, women reach Advanced Maternal Age (AMA) at thirty-five years old.[42] That means a woman is on the backside of her reproductive track once she reaches her late thirties. Men have similar issues as they age starting between thirty-five and forty-five, with a reduction in sperm viability, motility and mobility, and this starts to decline significantly around age fifty.[43] The takeaway being that for both sexes the risks of genetic abnormalities increase with age and the window between today's average age of getting married and/or conceiving is much closer to these reproductive declines.

GRAPHIC 3: **MONTHLY FERTILITY RATE BY AGE**

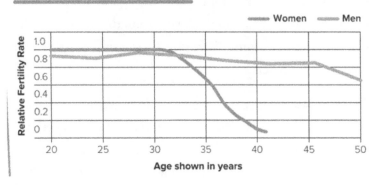

Also often heralded by the news media, are advances in fertility treatments that can help couples conceive well into their forties and beyond. Plus, advances in science and medicine give women a much higher chance of having a healthy pregnancy in their late thirties and forties. But there are limits, and many of these options are prohibitively expensive. A 2021 article published in Forbes magazine cited IVF costs at as much as $12,000 to $14,000 USD per attempt.[44]

Lots of women and men spend their twenties and early thirties gaining skills and/or an education, building a career, and collecting experiences. This popular trend shows no signs of abating and will very likely continue as life expectancy and standard of living continue to increase. Those who take this path often find themselves in their mid- to late-thirties wanting to have a child, but with no acceptable husband or wife prospects in the picture. The difficult question then becomes, am I going to force a "less-than-optimal" marriage to fulfill the proverbial "right way" which is effectively getting married "just to have a child" or are they going to have a child on their own? My premise is you should seriously explore being a parent within a Parenting Partnership as opposed to these two approaches.

Another data point is that people simply want to be "young parents" which allows them to have more varied experiences with their children, more time with their children and become grandparents at a reasonable age. By having a child at thirty-five through my first Parenting Partnership I seriously increased my chance of seeing my grandchildren by the time I am sixty-five or seventy. If I had skipped the Parenting Partner opportunity Anna offered me, and waited until I found my wife and had my first child at forty-seven, I would have had a smaller chance of seeing my grandchildren at age seventy-seven or later.

LGBTQ+ FAMILIES

Many LGBTQ+ couples have explored options to bring a child into the world with 24% of female same-sex couple raising a child and 8% of male same-sex couples raising kids. Additionally, 79% of these children are biological offspring with 21% being adopted children.[45] A recent article published by the BBC stated that, not only are more LGBTQ singles and couples hoping to expand their families, but many are considering asking friends and loved ones to act as sperm donors.[46] Some are inviting those sperm donors to be active participants in raising their child.

"Many queer couples seeking sperm want the experience to be personal, which means choosing to know who the sperm donor is. Several reasons drive this choice, such as knowing about the future child's biological parents, being in touch with them for medical questions and creating an extended family. While this is possible if a couple goes through a sperm bank or other type of connection service, choosing a friend or personal relation for the donation is less costly.

Regardless, these choices require a careful, deliberate thought process that involves emotional, financial and legal considerations that affect not just the lives of the parents and donors, but also those of their future children."

NEED TO HAVE A CHILD DUE TO MEDICAL ISSUES

Another reason for seeking a Parenting Partnership can be the early onset of reproductive health issues for females. The specifics causes are too numerous to list, but in general, reproductive health issues fall into three categories: naturally occurring, onset due to prolonged exposure to sexually transmitted disease, or stemming from medical complications from a failed pregnancy or abortion.

While these four motivations could stand on their own as a singular reason to initiate a Parenting Partnerships it is also likely that multiple factors, including some not listed here, would contribute to this very personal choice.

HOW WILL WE "DO IT"

Once you have decided to entertain the idea of a Parenting Partnership and you have an excellent Parenting Partner chosen, you'll need to have a slightly awkward, but absolutely required, conversation about how to "do it." How are we going to get a fertilized egg? Just as there are multiple parenting arrangements a child can be born into, there are multiple ways to fertilize an egg. Will you attempt to conceive by having sex or will you use other options available in our modern society? These two very different paths require significant conversation, planning and doctor visits that will likely both educate and test the resolve of each potential Parenting Partner.

Debating these possible paths, the physical requirements and financial costs associated with each will be a significant vetting step. Keep in mind that even if you can come to an agreement on an approach that works for both parties, both of you will need to get checked for fertility issues.

According to the Centers for Disease Control and Prevention, 6% of married women between the ages of fifteen and forty-four in the United States are infertile. Approximately 7.4

million U.S. women in this age group have used fertility services. In the United States, among heterosexual women aged fifteen to forty-nine years with no prior births, about one in five (19%) are unable to get pregnant after one year of trying, which is classed as infertility.[47] Also, about one in four (26%) women in this group have difficulty getting pregnant or carrying a pregnancy to term (impaired fecundity). For men The National Library of Medicine states, "The male is solely responsible in about 20% of cases and is a contributing factor in another 30% to 40% of all infertility cases. As male and female causes often co-exist, it is important that both partners are investigated for infertility and managed together."[48]

The following is a **very basic** pros and cons list for intercourse, intrauterine insemination (IUI), in vitro fertilization (IFV), surrogacy and adoption. As stated earlier, there are a multitude of books on these topics for you to further explore your options.

INTERCOURSE

Conceiving with your Parenting Partner through sexual activity.

PROS	CONS
• No medical/procedural intervention necessary	• Monogamy until conception
• No associated cost	• Potential exposure to STDs
• Accepted by all faiths/cultures[49]	• Pregnancy rate is 15-20% per cycle[50]
• Natural family planning information is easily accessible	• Unknown sperm/ egg quality
• Both parties make an equal time commitment	• Unknown genetic compatibility
• 90% of couples achieve pregnancy within a year	• Lifestyle changes to optimize conception rate[51]
	• Timing intercourse for ovulation is not exact
	• Irregular menstrual cycles lead to missed opportunities
	• Potential emotional complexity resulting from sexual interaction

INTRAUTERINE INSEMINATION (IUI)

Medical procedure delivering semen to the cervix or uterus.

PROS	CONS
• Less invasive and less expensive than IVF	• Average cost of sperm in the U.S. is $1000 per vial. This doesn't include the storage and shipping, or the insemination process which can add hundreds of dollars.[53]
• Biological child for the mother	
• Solves sperm issues: motility, mobility, abnormal morphology[52]	• Success rates 10% to 20% cycle[54]
• Can use partner or donor sperm	• If donor sperm, single parenthood with financial and emotional challenges
• Total parenting control if using a donor	• Your child having half siblings from donor sperm
• Can be done without additional medication/hormones	• A 2021 study out of Harvard noted 85% of people who discovered they were conceived through artificial insemination reported a "shift in their sense of self" and about half sought psychological help in order to cope.[55]
• Knowing the biological father's medical history	
• Possibly covered by insurance	• Sperm donor identity issues

IN VITRO FERTILIZATION (IVF)

Medical procedure where a woman's eggs and a man's sperm are combined outside the body to form embryos which are grown and then placed in the woman's uterus.

PROS	CONS
• 54% success rate in women under the age of thirty-five[56]	• Decreased success rate after maternal age thirty-five
• Women with ovarian failure/menopause/other issues can carry a child	• Significant chance of multiple births (twins, triplets, etc.)
• Can use partner or donor embryo/sperm	• Hormone injections and side effects
• Embryos can be screened for inherited diseases	• Multiple attempts can be required
• Can help diagnose fertilization problems	• One round of IVF can cost $15,000-$30,000 (including hormone injections and medication)[57]
	• Similar to IUI affects child's "sense of self" as above

SURROGACY

There are two types of surrogacy: traditional where the surrogate's egg is fertilized with the male partner's sperm and gestational where the surrogate carries the egg provided by partners. For the purposes of our book we will only be addressing gestational surrogacy where an embryo from the parenting partners is implanted.

PROS	CONS
• Genetic link to your child • Female partner does not have to gestate and deliver child • Involvement with surrogate from conception[58] • Confirmed healthy pregnancy: prenatal care participation, surrogate screening • Being able to raise a child even when you cannot biologically have one yourself • As opposed to adoption, full legal claim to child	• Cost: $80,000-$130,000, program fees, medical expenses, compensation[59] • Medical process for biological mother is similar to IVF process (high cost, hormones, procedure) • Lack of control over surrogates lifestyle, nutrition, health diligence • Surrogacy may not be viable, pregnancy complications • Emotional complexity • Legal complexity

ADOPTION

Legal process of becoming a non-biological parent by agreeing to take another's child and raising it as one's own.

PROS	CONS
• Raising a child when you cannot biologically have one	• The average cost of adoption in the United States is $70,000[61]
• Option of raising a child without a partner	• Biological parents can change their minds
• Helping children who do not yet have a parent	• Emotional adjustment period
• Choice of open or closed adoption[60]	• It can take up to a year for a domestic adoption and more for an international adoption[62]
• Choice of special needs, international adoption, transracial adoption, foster care, etc.	• Child's unknown medical history[63]
	• Complexities of child's extended family

IT'S ONE OF THE BETTER WAYS TO BRING A CHILD INTO THE WORLD

These past three chapters covered a lot of ground. Ultimately, when parents are partners rather than spouses, friends rather than lovers, they can consistently show the best of themselves to their child—instead of the worst. Parenting Partnerships allow parents to raise children in an emotionally stable, healthy, nurturing environment where both parents care for and respect each other, and work as a team to provide the best childhood possible. This idea is not only true in our personal experience, but is now being debated by relationships professionals such as Professor Susan Golombock of the University of Cambridge's Center for Family Research who states, "It is possible that taking away romantic baggage could make for a more stable environment."[64]

All relationships encounter challenges and go through ups and downs. Parenting Partnerships are not exempt from this. Sometimes we struggle, however, the major differentiator from a romantic relationship is that my partners and I have already laid the groundwork for such occasions. We've removed the romantic volatility by entering into a very structured agreement outlining values, boundaries and responsibilities before the children were even born. Like Profession Golombock indicates, the clear expectations and communication I've established with each Parenting Partner have created a loving and safe environment for each child where the focus is 100% on what is best for the child and not on the complex discrepancies between two intertwined adults.

Another last advantage of entering a Parenting Partnership is that it sets a higher bar for time prioritization and romantic love. In my case, I had a fulfilling single life with a solid career, close bonds with my family and friends and dating companionship. Fulfilling my strong desire for children through my Parenting Partnerships significantly enhanced my entire existence. Since my needs were met across the board, I no longer felt the need to "force a relationship" due to loneliness or pressure to "force a marriage" to have children. Instead, I was able to focus my time on the important priorities of being a dutiful father and driving forward in my career. Being in this peaceful state of higher level fulfillment helped me to avoid sub-par relationships and have the clarity to immediately identify and commit to my amazing partner. If I had not had my sons through my Parenting Partnerships I would have been tempted to settle into a less-than-optimal relationship and almost certainly missed out on deeper love.

CHAPTER 4

MY FIRST PARENTING PARTNERSHIP

I entered my first Parenting Partnership seventeen and a half years ago. It has been and continues to be a highly successful, life-changing decision that has brought me and my Parenting Partner Anna much joy. Our wonderful sixteen-year-old son Robert is happy, healthy, and totally loved by both his mother and father, extended family, half brothers, and stepmom. He's well adjusted with friends, enjoys extracurriculars, and makes great grades. He has a kind heart, works hard and exhibits a great attitude.

The origin of this Parenting Partnership is an interesting story and illustrates one of the many reasons a couple might consider a Parenting Partnership. While it's been a resounding success, I learned many lessons that I have applied to my second Parenting Partnership and marriage. I want to share those lessons with you, so you can make an educated decision and find your own success through a Parenting Partnership.

My first Parenting Partnership was not in my original life plan. It came about unexpectedly and caught me completely off guard. But with the circumstances being what they were, it made sense for both me and Anna.

AN UNEXPECTED PARTNERSHIP

In 2002, I was thirty years old and was moving from Detroit to Chicago to expand a startup business in six weeks. As luck would have it, that's when I met Anna, a twenty-six-year-old paralegal from a hard working immigrant background. We hit it off right away and began dating, despite the fact I would be leaving soon.

We got along great. I really liked her but I was leaving town, permanently. We continued to see each other even after I moved away. For about a year after I left Detroit, Anna and I had an on-again, off-again relationship.

Our relationship wasn't clearly defined or monogamous. Both of us were at a place in our lives where we didn't want to be tied down. We enjoyed each other's company and stayed in touch while living four hours away, until gradually the distance wore on us and the relationship dimmed and fizzled. By 2004, we had been off for some time.

About a year and a half after moving to Chicago, my business was doing great and I decided to relocate to Texas. A few months before the move, Anna came to Chicago for a visit. She was in town to see a friend and we decided to meet up. One thing led to another, and we ended up spending the night together. Maybe it was because we both saw this night as one last fling, but we were careless and had unprotected sex.

Little did I know that decision was about to change my life. About two months later, I got a phone call.

"Frank, I've had medical trouble, an ectopic pregnancy."

Obviously, it came as a tremendous shock to find out that Anna was facing a serious medical situation. It was an even greater surprise to learn the details of an ectopic pregnancy—that it is a dangerous and possibly life-threatening situation.[65]

In an ectopic pregnancy, the fertilized egg is stuck in the fallopian tubes, and while it's rare for a woman to die from this condition, it can still be very dangerous in societies without access to advanced medical procedures. Fortunately, Anna was surrounded by supportive family and excellent doctors whom she trusted. However, she quickly realized her life was going to be tremendously complicated by this medical difficulty.

Anna, only twenty-eight-years-old, developed serious health issues in the affected fallopian tube and ovary. Three months and many doctor visits later, specialists determined that one ovary was irreparably damaged from the ectopic pregnancy. They also found that she had severe endometriosis—a disorder in which tissue that normally lines the uterus grows outside the uterus—as one-third to one-half of women with this condition have difficulty getting pregnant and carrying a pregnancy to term.[66] Additionally, Anna was displaying a high risk for cervical cancer due to the recurrence of precancerous cells. The most devastating part was that the medical complications she suffered severely threatened her chances of someday becoming a mother, which was something she deeply desired.

After a year of tests, tentative diagnosis, and unsuccessful hormone treatments, the doctors did have some good news: Anna did not have cervical cancer. But there was also bad news. Her one and only window for conceiving a child was rapidly drawing to a close.

Anna called me as soon as the doctors broke the sad news to her. Due to the advancing endometriosis, the medical prognosis was that she had just six months to conceive and only three menstrual cycles in that window due to the damaged ovary. When that window of fertility closed, the doctors told her it would be closed for good and she'd never be able to conceive children. Basically, if Anna ever wanted to be a birthing mom, she would have to get pregnant very shortly after the hormone therapy wore off and before the endometriosis persisted.

Throughout this difficult time of loss, sadness, pain, doctor visits, hospital treatments and financial devastation, even though we were not a couple, I stayed involved. I helped Anna work through her options at each stage. I stood by as doctors prescribed various treatments and hormones to attempt to save the damaged ovary and restore her fertility. Nothing worked. It was now a medical certainty, she had very little time left to conceive a child.

THE BIG ASK

Despite being totally caught off guard by the medical prognosis, after the shock wore off Anna, now twenty-nine, was surprisingly positive and logical about her options. One of her options, it turned out, was me.

Even though we weren't romantically involved at that point, I was deeply invested in Anna and wanted to do anything I could to help her. I offered assistance with her medical expenses and stayed in close contact with her throughout her medical treatments and afterward. Still, nothing prepared me for the surprise of what she was about to ask.

At the time this all began, Anna was a university student pursuing a second degree in biology, which meant she no longer had health insurance through an employer and was too old to be on her parents' insurance. Though she had considerable savings from her previous jobs, the medical bills hit her hard financially, and the fear of never having children drained her emotionally.

Running out of time, and not having anyone special in her life at that moment, she asked me if I would have a child with her. Not get married. Not be romantically involved. Just conceive and raise a child together... as partners.

Once I realized she was starkly serious, I was stunned. Not only was this an incredible and unusual ask, but I had to make a decision fast. She was running out of time.

FATHER FIGURE? ME?

I couldn't help but feel honored by Anna's request to have a child with her. I also realized I'd been asked to make a life-altering decision and had a lot to think about.

The decision was a difficult one because I really wanted to help her. I knew she'd be a wonderful mother and it saddened me to think that Anna would never have children. But was I ready for fatherhood? Was I mature enough? Was this the right move for me? I felt I owed it to her to at least consider her proposal.

On one hand, it had always been a goal of mine to be a dad. I have two brothers who are fifteen and seventeen years younger than me, and I always loved spending time with them in a quasi-parental role. I'd always known having kids would be part of my life plan, but at that time I wasn't living a lifestyle geared toward marriage and family. Rather, I was focused on building my career, experiencing life, and being actively single.

My new business kept me busy and often on the road. In addition, not only had I just moved to a new city, but I was also dating someone else at that point. There were plenty of reasons to keep my life just the way it was. Why change everything by making a life-altering commitment right then?

DEEP INTROSPECTION

Anna's request forced me to think about the timeline of my life in a way I had not previously done before. What was my long-term plan? Was I even the marrying type? If so, was I likely to get married anytime soon? If marrying later, there was not any guarantee that my spouse would want to have kids or be able to conceive? This whole situation caused me to do some serious introspection and reflection on my past, present and potential prospects as I was still waiting to meet the right person with whom to settle down. Anna's request accelerated and deepened my reflective process.

It didn't help that at that point in my life I was seeing many of the marriages around me begin to show signs of unhealthy attributes. I had witnessed divorce among friends and business associates, as well as within my extended family. Even my parents, who have now been together for fifty-four years, had two full years of separation (along with rough years before and after) during my mid childhood—an event that was painful for me and my sister, who is two years younger. My parents' marital problems left me shaken, but not completely jaded about getting married. While I knew I didn't want a marriage exactly like theirs, it was an overall good marriage and I had witnessed other positive examples of marriage in my extended family. On my mother's side, everyone is married. They don't get divorced. They had widows and couples in marriages. On my dad's side, there are multiple divorces and multiple half siblings. Some second marriages lasted and were healthy examples. My cousins from these varied marriages, and even my own siblings, have all turned out very differently with some from divorce situations being more well-adjusted than those who had a stable home life with married parents.

Positive takeaways from this cross-section of marriages were that families take many shapes, half sibling can be a full sibling in your heart and that even two year separations can be overcome. Negative realizations were likely the same as what you the reader have experienced, that marriages between two people with plenty of chemistry, shared interest, and the best of intentions can fizzle with negative ramifications for them and their offspring. So, at thirty-three, much like many of you, I wasn't feeling sure that long-term marriage was a great option for me personally or that it would happen for me.

Even though I knew I had a strong desire for children, I had to reflect upon what kind of parenting I had experienced and the type of parent I aspired to be. I had to look carefully at my own character. While everyone has positives and negatives to their personality, some character traits are better suited for parenting than others. For example, my clarity of vision, generous spirit and sense of optimism seemed like strong points in favor of me being a solid parent. On the other hand, I can lack patience and abhor routine, both of which are required to parent at a high level. Would I be willing to change my priorities, habits and improve my weaknesses? One of the most important attributes of a good parent is a willingness to put time and effort into improving yourself. Not only is it beneficial to you and your family, but as a bonus, it's a great trait to pass on to your kids.

Lastly, I tried to decouple my feelings about the societal and religious dictate to get married first before having kids versus what I had seen of marriage within my extended family and

Anna's proposal. The problem was, while I might have been ready to become a father, I certainly was not ready to get married to anyone I had in my life at the time. Furthermore, I still felt like I had some time to fall in love, get married and start a family the traditional way. I worry, if we had a child together it would make future dating complicated for each of us and maybe diminish the chances of finding true love and getting married. For all these reasons, even though I knew it would crush her, my initial answer to Anna was no. I encouraged her to explore all her other options.

STRANGE ULTIMATUM

Despite a difficult medical situation and the disappointment of me turning down her offer, Anna was very strong and optimistic in how she handled everything. Can you imagine being told you have a deadline on your reproductivity?

Anna and I both understood that many married couples are given similar devastating news when trying to have a baby. They often turn to other methods of conception, most of which I shared in the previous chapter. After doing some research, I sat down to go over all the possible scenarios with Anna. I didn't know how she'd respond to this information, but to her credit, Anna didn't ignore my suggestions and took time to research and think about all of them. Ultimately, she took issue with each of the options I had put forth.

I distinctly remember our follow-up conversation a few months later when she explained with passion why those other options didn't work for her. She very much wanted to have *her own biological child*—her own flesh and blood—which ruled out adoption. She didn't have any other close friend that she could envision as the father of her child. There simply wasn't anyone else in her life she fully trusted in that way.

As for the remaining options, the medical bills had left her finances completely drained. She didn't have the money to fund an alternative method of conceiving, or to freeze her eggs—which can cost tens of thousands of dollars. In other words, it was either me or no children at all. Ever.

TIME TO RECONSIDER

Anna's situation weighed on me and I couldn't simply turn her down again and fade out of her life without giving her the respect of seriously exploring my heart and soul. I also felt somewhat responsible for what happened to her medically, as I had been her last sexual partner. I empathized with the unimaginable shock and suffering she'd been through.

When you are in your early thirties—especially as a man—you don't really think about reproductive issues. I wasn't married. I wasn't even dating seriously. I know married couples who hadn't thought seriously about these topics. Nobody ever thinks it's going to happen to them or to someone they love. When Anna was first diagnosed with her ectopic pregnancy and was told that her ovary was extremely damaged, I made an effort to learn about reproductive issues. During the year she was going through her hormone treatments, we were both really hopeful this option would work for her and that she'd have a long, healthy reproductive window. Turns out, this wasn't the case. When she asked me a second time to consider becoming her Parenting Partner, I knew this was her final opportunity to become a mother. I was touched that she wanted to share the experience with me.

A Parenting Partnership was beginning to make sense to me. From her perspective, it was the only option left for her to have a child. Her chances of becoming a biological mother were fast approaching an untimely end. She didn't have the luxury of waiting several years to get married to an ideal match. If she wanted to have a child, it had to happen quickly. In her view, I was the best person for the role.

When I realized Anna considered me to be the best (and only) option to actualize her dream of becoming a mother, I knew I owed it to her to reconsider. I began to visualize how the arrangement might work and tried to think through the potential challenges and benefits that would likely arise.

WHAT CHANGED MY MIND

Up until Anna asked me to father a child with her, I always assumed I would wait until I was married to have a family, probably in my late-thirties or forties—or maybe even my fifties. Now for the first time I began to think about some of the repercussions of that idea. Putting off marriage and children until your forties or fifties means accepting the increased chances that your chosen romantic partner may already have kids and may not want to have more children with you, and there may be added challenges around getting pregnant and bringing that pregnancy to term.

When Anna came to me, I was forced to determine the priority of having kids in my life. I asked myself what type of dad I wanted to be and what kind of parenting experience I wanted to have. Asking myself all these questions was more than a soul-searching exercise. Without realizing it, I was decoupling the concept of parenting from the concept of marriage. For the first time, I saw that they don't have to go hand-in-hand.

I began to seriously consider Anna's proposal.

For most of my life, I thought that when I eventually started a family, I would follow the same traditional path as my parents. Breaking from that tradition didn't scare me. Mainly because I had witnessed many divorces and the co-parenting situations of friends, coworkers and my father's side of the family. Once I'd decided I was fine with decoupling marriage from child-rearing, I began to explore the important aspects of raising a child with someone I was not romantically involved with, and how we could accomplish successful parenting outside of marriage.

CHANGE OF HEART

The idea was beginning to make sense to me. I started to think through all the details that would have to be present to make this work. What would this relationship look like exactly? How would we manage it day to day? Do we need legal documents? What would other people think? What's the worst that could happen?

I knew that I did not want to get married just for the purpose of having a child, as some couples do. That was not for me.

I realized that if we were going to conceive and parent a child together in a sort of partnership without being married or even romantically involved, we would have to create a new model from scratch. Parenting Partnerships are unconventional now, but at that time they were practically unheard of.

It wasn't as though we were completely unprepared for what we were considering. We were both mature adults. I knew Anna and I had each experienced a lot in life, and we both felt ready to become parents.

Creating this new family model wasn't as daunting for me as it could have been. In addition to having a big heart and a lot of enthusiasm, I consider myself an analytical thinker and a skilled problem solver. The prospect of raising a child with someone I respected and admired was exciting and intriguing. But I also knew that what mattered most was how this sort of nontraditional family situation would affect *the child*.

There too, I was confident in our approach. Did I personally want to have a child? Yes. Did Anna want a child? Yes. Did I think Anna would be a great mother? Yes. Did I think I would be a committed, loving father? Absolutely. To me, those were the four most important questions. Knowing those four things is the foundation for any couple planning to have children. The decision to have a child is not a frivolous one. It's a lifetime commitment.

PARENTING PIONEERS

Looking back I now realize that Anna and I were at a pivotal point in social history; we were contemplating a new family paradigm personally and culturally. If we decided to do this, we were going to come up with a totally new approach to creating a family—something we'd never seen before.

Despite the challenges, I was confident that with the right commitment and the right guidelines, we could make this unconventional situation work really well. Most importantly, I was confident that by partnering with Anna the two of us could raise an amazing child who would be surrounded by love and affection and would thrive with us as parents.

Both my heart and mind were ready to say yes, but I knew there was so much more to discuss. Ultimately, it took a year and a half for me to make the decision to enter a Parenting Partnership with Anna.

ANNA'S TIMELINE

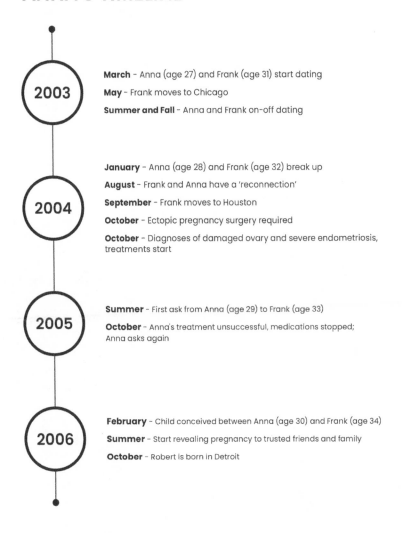

March - Anna (age 27) and Frank (age 31) start dating

May - Frank moves to Chicago

Summer and Fall - Anna and Frank on-off dating

2003

January - Anna (age 28) and Frank (age 32) break up

August - Frank and Anna have a 'reconnection'

September - Frank moves to Houston

October - Ectopic pregnancy surgery required

October - Diagnoses of damaged ovary and severe endometriosis, treatments start

2004

Summer - First ask from Anna (age 29) to Frank (age 33)

October - Anna's treatment unsuccessful, medications stopped; Anna asks again

2005

February - Child conceived between Anna (age 30) and Frank (age 34)

Summer - Start revealing pregnancy to trusted friends and family

October - Robert is born in Detroit

2006

CHAPTER 5

PARENTING PARTNERSHIP FORMATION BASICS

Now that you have heard the beginning of my and Anna's story, what is your story? Where are you on your path to becoming a parent? At what point in your life would your desire to become a parent overtake your preference for living a single life or holding out for a Good | Great | Awesome Marriage to have a child in the traditional way? Who would you ask to be your Parenting Partner if you had to choose someone immediately?

There are four crucial KEY POINTS FOR A PARENTING PARTNERSHIP to form:

1. Deep desire to be a parent and knowing the time is right for you

2. Connecting with someone you respect who deeply desires to be a parent and is ready to commit

3. Creating your legal documents and Shared Expectations Document across all important aspects of parenting

4. Being able to conceive a child and complete a pregnancy

These next few chapters will focus on key points 1, 2 and 3 above.

Having a child will change your entire life. Becoming a father changed my outlook and day-to-day life in a much greater way than getting married did. Ask others in your life which was more impactful and a greater change in their outlook and existence—marriage or children.

While people can debate if a Parenting Partnership is as emotionally or legally binding as a marriage, it no doubt requires a similar amount of effort, agreement, understanding, and maturity between the partners. Furthermore, the person you have a child with will be intertwined in your life for at least twenty years or more and you will have a long tail of ongoing interactions with them for almost all of your existence. This is, in some ways, a much more significant commitment than a modern marriage, which sometimes ends in a matter of days through an annulment, or after a few years through a divorce. As family court judge Lawrence R. Jones wrote in his article *Platonic Parenting: An emerging concept in an ever changing world,* "A party who enters into such a platonic parenting agreement must understand that they may be assuming a lifetime of co-parenting with the platonic partner, just as if they had a more traditional parenting relationship."[67]

This decision should be held in the highest of regard by both partners and entered into only after much forethought and soul searching.

KEY POINT #1

DEEPLY DESIRING FROM A HEALTHY, HAPPY PLACE AT THE RIGHT TIME

Where to start this soul searching? How about with the ever-present and always applicable question—*are you happy with yourself?* This eternal question and your answer applies to Parenting Partnerships the same as it does to everyday existence and preparedness for romantic relationships. You need to be happy and healthy within yourself first. Many members of society are managing addiction, mental illness or life-threatening physical illnesses which would require special consideration before moving forward with a proposed Parenting Partner. Starting this journey without a thorough discussion and plan for these struggles would not be fair to yourself, your potential Parenting Partner or to the child you are bringing into the world.

If each partner is in a positive place, the next step is to determine each partner's desire to be a parent. Desiring children, much like marriage, is in decline as well. When Pew Research asked adults without children who were aged eighteen to forty-nine if they were likely to have kids, 56% were child positive, but 44% said they were "not too likely" or "not at all likely" to have kids. Half of these respondents stated they were "just not wanting to have children."[68] So simply assuming other unmarried, single people want to have kids is not at all a given. It would also not be advisable to enter into a Parenting Partnerships with someone who "maybe" wants kids. You need to find a potential partner that deeply desires to be a parent. Make sure you fall into this category as well.

Assuming you have a deep desire to have a child of your own, what are the reasons and motivations for that deep desire? Make sure they are all healthy in nature and coming from a place of positivity. If either partner's reasons for having a child is because "I am lonely," or "to make me happy," or "because I can"—those are red flags that need to be taken seriously and investigated vigorously.

The next step is to determine if the timing is right for both partners. Someone could be perfectly happy in their existence, have a deep desire for children, but it may not be the right time for them for a litany of reasons. As for timing, there are many quotes that trumpet the fact that "no one is ever ready to become a parent," but often with Parenting Partnerships you can choose to pick a time in your life when you are as close to ready as possible. Seeing as most Parenting Partnerships will be initiated by people in their thirties and forties, career and financial concerns will likely be the biggest issues when determining if the timing is right for both partners. While Anna had a true need to have a child quickly, she did ask me at an age and time when I felt very prepared to take the step into parenthood.

KEY POINT #2

MUTUAL RESPECT, COMMUNICATION AND ALIGNMENT

The three items of Key Point #1 are very straightforward—being healthy and happy with oneself, having a deep desire to have children and being at the right time in your life to commit. The aspects to finding a Parenting Partner are more complicated. Your Parenting Partner needs to be someone with whom you share mutual respect, with whom you have healthy communication, and with whom your values align. Many people may meet the first three personal qualifiers, but these fourth, fifth and sixth metrics are very unique to the dynamic between the two individuals.

In what way do we mean mutual respect? Respect that we believe the potential partners have the qualities to be, and are deeply committed to being, an excellent parent in a way that resonates with the other partner. Are they positive, patient, kind, giving, nurturing, responsible, and do they value family? Are they willing to completely change the life they are presently enjoying to devote a large portion of their life to being the best parent they can possibly be? Will each of you be a good, reliable partner to the other?

Communication is key in all relationships. You will need to assess how well you can communicate with your Parenting Partner, especially in distressing situations. Can you communicate clearly and respectfully when things get tough, when you don't agree, or when a crisis strikes? Can you set proper communication boundaries and do you share a common desire and commitment to honest and positive communications?

The last portion is alignment of values between the partners. Do you and your potential partner agree on the core issues of parenting and how your child will be raised, or do you have differing viewpoints on many issues? (This important topic will be covered in greater detail in the next two chapters.)

Here's a personal test—review the most serious and significant friendships and romantic partners you've had in your life. Take the time to debate if they would meet your criteria for becoming a Parenting Partner. How do they stack up compared to the person who you are debating having a child with at present?

There are a number of people with whom I was great friends or had dated semi-seriously or seriously that I would not have had a child with because they would not have met many of these criteria. Some great friends and past girlfriends would have gotten a resounding "No" if they had asked me to be their

Parenting Partner. I always knew in my heart that Anna was a mature, fundamentally good person and would be both a great parent and a good partner for me. I deeply respected her ability to be a devoted mother which made the decision much easier than it might have been, and it has informed our relationship to this day. When I called Anna to tell her I was possibly ready to move forward, she was thrilled. However, in order for me to get involved in a Parenting Partnership, we needed to make sure there were no deal breakers for the two of us, and that on a deeper level our values and expectations aligned.

When getting married, many aspects are assumed. Parenting Partnerships turn these and other assumptions into matters of discussion—which may reveal some deal breakers early on. For Anna and I, these deal breakers included topics such as:

- Reconciling geographic location as she was in Michigan and I was in Texas
- Equitable sharing of time with our child, allowing us both to be involved parents
- Establishing a detailed financial agreement
- Religious and naming considerations

What would be possible deal breakers with your top three potential Parenting Partners?

Beyond these first deal breakers, we needed to work through our ground rules and a shared set of expectations. How would we make decisions? How would we handle disagreements? How would we share time with our child? Where would our child stay throughout the week? Who would pay for what? What non-ordinary parenting theories did either of us harbor? And dozens of other important questions. Without those numerous and deep preliminary discussions, I can't imagine our Parenting Partnership would have been successful over the past seventeen years.

The next two chapters will walk you through what should be included in your legal documents which establish the bare minimum floor responsibilities for each partner, and your Shared Expectations Document which outlines what each partner *wants, expects and is willing to offer in addition to the minimum commitment* as a Parenting Partner. Both are crucial to establish before you start trying to conceive your child.

CHAPTER 6

ESTABLISHING IMPORTANT LEGAL DOCUMENTS

With each of my Parenting Partners, I've established two separate types of documents—legal documents as required by law and a Shared Expectations Document which has no legal standing but is equally—if not more—important. These documents make up Key Point #3 and are another major milestone for you and your potential Parenting Partner. This chapter will cover the government standard, required legal documents to establish agreed upon custody, with the next chapter exploring the Shared Expectations Document.

Some examples for clarity between the two types of documents. The state requires your child to have a name, but does not care what you name your child, whereas you and your

Parenting Partner very much do. The state does not dictate what approaches to discipline will be used with your child, or precisely what type of education they will receive, but you and your Parenting Partner will have strong opinions based on your past experiences that need to be communicated and agreed upon. The state dictates that child support payments must be made, but not exactly how child support payments are spent. Requirements versus approaches.

PUT IT IN WRITING

According to legal experts, a written agreement can serve as a road map, helping each parent navigate their role as caregiver. The agreement offers tangible guidance when difficult and emotional decisions arise.[69] It also works as a backstop should arguments escalate so that threats cannot be made and so that negative actions will have consequences. Think of the legal documents as the base level responsibilities and minimum amount of cooperation between Parenting Partners. These tenets are governed by the laws of your jurisdiction. These are the requirements and boundaries *you are legally required to follow as a parent* if in the future you and your Parenting Partner aren't able to work together one-on-one in a positive manner. You'll need to meet with a family lawyer to draft and file these documents. While this may sound negative, the point of many legal documents is not to outline interactions when all goes well, but to set the "guardrails and the floor" for when situations have degraded.

Legal documents are involved for a variety of important reasons but mostly to assure three attributes: financial contribution, location of child's home and custody time for each parent. Without paternal acknowledgment full custody is awarded to the mother. This 100% maternal custody default should be avoided as that is not why either party is pursuing a Parenting Partnership.

A parental legal agreement is set for the first eighteen years of the child's life. Note that at age twelve or a couple of years later the child will have a say in how they want to spend their time. This is both a legal fact and a parenting reality. Additionally, some aspects of the legal agreement will likely live on through high school graduation which may be more than eighteen years.[70]

Anna and I worked with a family lawyer and spent a lot of time discussing what to put into our legal agreements. We crafted it together and came up with a document which has worked well for us for seventeen years. I'm thankful that I've never had to go to court or even engage lawyers to overcome any difficulties. We attribute this to thorough pre-planning discussions.

In both of my Parenting Partnerships we operate well above the required arrangements for scheduling flexibility, holiday times, vacation arrangements, educational efforts, health insurance and providing more monthly financial resources than required in the legal documents. It is my strong suggestion that you should allow yourself leeway to do the same, meaning don't legally bind yourself to the maximum commitments *you want to make*, instead legally commit to the basic commitments *you can definitely make.*

WHAT'S THE WORST THAT CAN HAPPEN?

Make sure you have a few hours to hear all the horror stories before you ask a family attorney, "What's the worst that can happen?" Any experienced, reputable family law attorney will be well aware of the possible downsides and be able to give you sage advice. Additionally, your attorney can provide boilerplate documents applicable to your jurisdiction that will make it a relatively easy process. Your legal documents are designed to create legal barriers to protect both parties and the child from worst-case scenarios. It might sound harsh and unpleasant, but it's critical to maintaining a respectful relationship with your partner. Formal legal agreements are not meant to set the tone for your relationship with your Parenting Partner and ideally can be kept locked away in a file cabinet and not pulled out unless absolutely necessary.

I strongly believe our legal documents provided Anna and I with significant peace of mind during any disagreements. Shortly after having our child, I had bouts of an irrational fear that Anna would run off and take our child to a remote location where I would never see him. Anna also had unfounded fears that I would end my financial support or cut ties. Having a legally binding agreement severely diminished those unfounded fears for both of us and allowed us to move forward with confidence. We both know exactly what is required in those legal documents, and we have no interest (or leverage) in trying to renegotiate custody, finances or any other section. Instead, whenever there's a matter of disagreement, we work together toward a solution. We both know that if push ever came to shove, the terms of the written legal agreement would prevail and could be enforced. And we agree that a battle in the courts is a last resort that likely will not be beneficial for anyone involved.

Conceiving parents who haven't worked out a legal document for financial and custody arrangements don't even have a baseline agreement which I would imagine is very disconcerting. Say, for example, a few years into a Parenting Partnership with no custody agreement, your partner asks for more financial support, which you then decline to give. In response, they pick up your child from school and leave for the weekend depriving you of time with your child. You would rightly be very, very upset, but without a legal agreement in place you would have no real recourse. Trust would erode and things could devolve.

If you aren't doing Parenting Partnership right then you may experience any of the following very unpleasant situations: visits from child protective services (CPS), mandated counseling, supervised visitations, court battles, judges determining aspects of your parenting life and the police being called. I'm so thankful to report that we've never had any of these experiences, but sadly know of some families that have.

Before you start preparing your legal agreement for a Parenting Partnership, consider the following:

- Your custody agreement isn't meant to replace good communication. Your custody arrangement won't detail precisely where and when a child is to be picked up and dropped off, for example. It's only meant to provide a baseline expectation for both parties that ensures neither party feels threatened by having their child taken away from them or being financially abandoned.

- Your agreement should be created and agreed to *before conception of the child*. The worst thing would be to start a pregnancy only to have one of the partners refuse to sign an agreement or try to renegotiate different terms. By preparing these documents and asking your partner to agree to them *before* getting pregnant, you can ascertain that the other person is serious about their commitment and intends to live up to it. Also, a written document should be clear and concise, leaving no room for interpretation. Lastly, ask your attorney when would be the best time to sign—prior to attempting, after confirmation of successful start of pregnancy, after pregnancy is viable, or after birth.

- While you should agree to all terms of the arrangement prior to conception, make sure your partnership agreement only becomes legally binding once the child is born. Work with your attorney to determine the proper approach for your jurisdiction.

CUSTODY AGREEMENT

It might sound daunting to create a custody arrangement, but it's really not. There's little you need to make up on your own as custody arrangements follow a state-regulated formula. I recommend partners agree upon and share one family attorney; two attorneys may create the exact kind of conflict you want to avoid—not to mention double your bill.

If you don't feel quite ready to speak to a lawyer, your state regulations on shared custody and parental finances can easily be researched on the internet. Remember that the figures for child support posted online are usually minimums and only a fraction of what you'll ultimately spend if you want to be an active parent providing for your child. Children are expensive. For 2022 it was projected that middle income parents spend an average of $272,049 over eighteen years, not including higher education which can cost upwards of one hundred thousand dollars.[71] Housing and food are the largest expenses with childcare being the biggest wildcard. Expensive metros like New York City and San Francisco project to be well over $500,000 for a child.[72]

You can expect that your shared financial obligations will depend on the contributing partner's taxable income. For example, if you make $36,000 per year the state will probably mandate a minimum of around $350 per month. If you make $50,000 per year then it might be $720 per month. $100,000 a year would require nearly $1,500 of monthly support. You should be able to find an online calculator specific to your state that estimates monthly child support payments that factor in your salary and whether or not you are providing insurance coverage. As a guideline, child support payments are typically 15% of the non-custodial parent's average monthly net resources. These details vary significantly based on the partnership and generally factor joint custody and equitable sharing of the child's time. We address finances again later on, but suffice to say contribution amounts are negotiable and will depend on the career plans of the two partners.

I suppose someone could attempt to negotiate their state-required financial support down. However, an action like that indicates a lack of commitment to be a supportive parent. If 15% of your pay seems high then you may want to take a hard look at your finances, consult with a free financial planning service, and evaluate and restructure your lifestyle to accommodate the added expenses of you becoming a parent. Financial concerns are a real reason that many people cite for not having children. As parents you'll likely spend more than this state allotted/dictated/enforced amount once all costs are considered. Children are always expensive and can be even more so in urban settings.

The legal documents will include how many days per week each parent will have the child in their care, as well as general rules for how travel, holidays, and vacations will be handled. These discussions are a good way of assuring that each partner is willing and able to make the compromises needed to have a fair partnership that supports the child. It also helps both sides feel comfortable that they will get what they need from the partnership, regardless of whether or not the two parents are getting along perfectly.

You can certainly make changes and amendments to the custody agreement after it's signed and the child is born, but only if both partners agree. For example, Parenting Partners may agree before the baby's birth that the father will see the child according to a standard, "every other weekend, plus Thursdays" type arrangement. However, once the child reaches a certain age, either parent may want to revisit that arrangement. Perhaps one parent wants to coach the child's Tuesday night sports practice, and it makes more sense for the child to stay at that parents house overnight instead of just spending two hours together on a Thursday night. If the mother sees the rationale here, the two can revise their agreement with their lawyer and submit to a family court judge who will generally allow it. While this is a benign example and one that doesn't require the lawyers and court to get involved, these kinds of changes can be made if needed. As long as both parties are in agreement, you can petition the court to make any changes to your agreement that you wish. Once both parties have signed and executed the legally binding document, it is an enforceable contract.

Custody agreements are filed with the court in accordance with state law. Keep in mind the state's main concern is the child. The judge is not interested in the details of your business or the traffic that makes you late for your pick-up and drop-off. What they are looking for is an arrangement that ensures the child is in a healthy environment and is being physically, emotionally, and financially looked after.

The state's seriousness surrounding custody issues is another reason it's advisable to involve an experienced lawyer in creating your agreement. While you can probably find standard forms through LegalZoom and other online resources, if you attempt to file a document with the court that doesn't make sense or doesn't adequately cover your situation in accordance with state law, it will likely get rejected by a judge. Not only can a lawyer advise you and answer most of your questions about this process, but they can also work their legal wordsmith magic to ensure your agreement is airtight. If you try to do it yourself, you may end up with loopholes that leave you or your partner's rights exposed.

It is likely that some discussions around your custody agreement will be sensitive for you or your Parenting Partner. Another advantage of having a family lawyer involved is their experience in acting as a mediator between two parties. Family lawyers are skilled at diplomatically negotiating in everyone's best interests. They can also present both partners with examples of worst-case scenarios that you might not have even thought of, and then help you craft your agreement in a way that ensures both parties' protection and peace of mind.

Involving a lawyer in your custody agreement also helps in spotting potential red flags. Having been through the custody process hundreds of times before, a good family lawyer will be able to recognize the signs of a partner who is less serious or reliable than a parent should be. If you start to feel uncomfortable with your partner at any stage in the negotiation process, it's time to seriously consider whether or not that partner is someone you want to work closely with for the next two decades.

Your attorney will walk you through options on the following items:

I. PRECISE CUSTODY OPTIONS

There is differing verbiage used across different jurisdictions, so you'll hear terms such as "conservatorship", "visitation", "possession order", "physical" etc.... and also "joint"or "sole" custody. For the purposes of this book we suggest "joint legal custody" which gives both parents rights to have input on all important decisions dealing with medical, educational, religious, visitation, and location.[73]

2. CHILD SUPPORT

A standard custody agreement creates certain obligations for each parent in the partnership. One obligation that is mandatory in many states is contributing to a state-supervised child support program. Child support payments must go through the state to be properly documented. Making child support payments directly to a partner will not be recognized by the state and can ultimately end in default, back payments, and a warrant for arrest. It is imperative to work through the state-supervised program to make your child support payments. This is to provide accountability and prevent both misuse of funds and false allegations of non-payment.

Anecdotally, many of us have heard or read horror stories about people paying alimony directly to their ex and the ex claiming they were never paid. Even if you show proper bank records indicating the money was sent to your partner, you can't always prove that money was intended for child support. Having the child support check go through the state means you can be sure the state has a record that you've actually fulfilled your obligation. It's unfortunate that such a system has to exist, but it does keep everyone honest.

Beyond the monthly payments, I also recommend that Parenting Partners set up a separate checking account for all child expenses. This account would receive the monthly child support payment and monthly contributions from the Parenting Partners above and beyond what is required by the custody agreement. The account would be viewable by both partners, accessible by debit cards, and only used for agreed upon expenses. This clarifies finances for both parties and makes child-related expenses easily trackable.

I cannot stress enough how imperative it is to have legal documents covering financial and custody arrangements negotiated before entering into a Parenting Partnership. It serves to protect the custodial parents from a partner who decides not to contribute financially and protects a non-custodial parent from not getting time with their child or worse. Also, many of these outrageous cases involve "known sperm donor" scenarios not handled through a sperm bank. A strategy that while easy and inexpensive, is rife with issues.

SPERM DONOR - LESBIAN COUPLE

Married mechanic who fosters kids in Topeka, Kansas responds to a Craig's List offer of $50 to be a sperm donor for a lesbian couple's artificial insemination. He has virtually no contact with the child, has no parental rights and an agreement with the mother to never have to pay support. When the mother breaks up with her girlfriend and applies for social assistance, the state then tracks him down to pay years worth of child support. Eventually a judge did rule in his favor.

https://www.cnn.com/2014/01/23/justice/kansas-sperm-donation/index.html

SPERM DONOR - NON-COUPLED

According to a National Post report, the two met as medical students in 1991. Both graduated and became MDs. In 2000, the woman, Dr. Amie Cullimore, contacted her old friend, Dr. Michael Ranson, and asked him to make good on a promise made nearly a decade earlier, to donate his sperm so that she could become a mother. She subsequently had two children via in vitro fertilization, or IVF, using Ranson's sperm. Ranson, who had no plans to become a father, agreed to stay in contact with the children, who are now teens. Following the birth of the second child in 2002, Cullimore and Ranson signed an agreement stating that she would have full custody of the children and would not seek financial support from Ranson. He remained in contact with the children, spent time with them as his extended family, paid for visits with his family and trips to Disneyland, and in 2011 provided $22,000 to Cullimore to help cover expenses and create a college fund for the kids. Now Cullimore is basing her suit, in part, on the fact that Ranson has acted as a father to the children.

In 2015 she sued Ranson for child support, saying she could no longer afford the $800 per month cost of child care. If she prevails, Ranson will be on the hook for child care payments, retroactive to 2012, as well as other expenses, including a portion of the children's education costs. According to the National Post, "Cullimore makes just under $250,000 a year as a gynecologist, obstetrician and university professor… while Ranson made just under CAD$280,000 in his most recent post with the World Bank in Europe."

Commenting on this particular case, attorney Richard Vaughn the founder of International Fertility Law Group wrote, "The Canadian case also points to the misperception of many intended parents that using a friend or family member to provide sperm lessens the need for a strong legal agreement. In fact, using friends or family as donors or surrogates *increases* the need for a strong agreement that clearly states the rights and responsibilities of all parties. A family member or acquaintance may have a different perception of his or her parental status than the intended parents, or future conflicts could arise that would make a mutual understanding meaningless. The best way to protect the parental rights of intended parents, the well-being of the child, and the intentions of the donor is to get it in writing—in the form of a properly executed legal agreement in compliance with the laws of the relevant jurisdiction."

https://www.iflg.net/
canadian-sperm-donor-sued-child-support/

CUSTODIAL FATHER ATTEMPTS TO DISASSOCIATE THE BIOLOGICAL MOTHER

A couple gets divorced and custody of the son is granted to the biological father, David. Nanci, the biological mother, was named a managing conservator but was not ordered to pay child support. David eventually remarried and attempted termination of the conservatorship between Nanci Holley and her son. "During the trial, David testified that he brought the termination suit because if he had died, he thought it would be better for his wife (the child's stepmother) to raise the child rather than Nanci (the biological mother)."

The Court ruled against this, but the case set a new precedent of using careful analysis of the "best interest of the child" standard in Texas, called the "Holley Factors".

https://www.langleybanack.com/
top-family-law-cases-holley-adams/

COPARENTING CUSTODY

Divorcees coparenting. ER Physician mother loses custody of four-year old due to dad's claim of Covid fears...

https://www.sheknows.com/
parenting/articles/2218078/
doctor-coronavirus-custody-co-parenting/

...don't have parental rights, your child can be adopted by someone else without your permission.

3. HOUSING AND MOVES

Following the agreed upon weekly custody plan, Parenting Partners need to consider what they will do about the homes in which their child is raised. Will they buy or rent their homes? What are acceptable living quarters for the child? Are they OK with a Parenting Partner living with extended family in the house? What about roommates? Will they work together to buy a home that will be given to the child in the future? It's important to consider the long-term ramifications of how you will handle your child's primary home. Since state laws vary, an experienced family lawyer can advise you on this subject. But you need to think about it in advance.

Another very important aspect is agreeing to live long term in a very specific geographic area which will be specified in the legal documents. Normally this names the jurisdiction where the custody agreement is filed and the adjoining counties as possible locations for residence. Be sure to factor in how your location will impact the partners job opportunities or conversely inhibit a partner moving for any variety of reasons: to support relatives during a time of need, wanting to "move back home", to be closer to a romantic interest, or wanting to try a different location.

4. VACATIONS AND HOLIDAYS

Think back to your childhood. Do you remember any random Tuesday's or do you, like most of us, mostly remember the special festivities and family trips? Dividing up the vacations and holidays that create these memories is very important. Discussions can get very emotionally charged as these special opportunities are inherently intertwined with each parent wanting to pass on traditions, attend extended family gatherings and maximize time with their child while off from work. Add in possible travel complexities and financial obligations and it can get prickly quickly. Shorter three day weekends are usually easier to manage. From year to year, holidays and school breaks fall on different weeks and days which can require the partners to adjust outside of the strict standards of the legal documents. The legal document will usually outline a division of holidays on a yearly basis which then alternates every other year. Example: if a parent gets Thanksgiving this year they don't get Christmas, then next year they get Christmas, but not Thanksgiving.

You'll have a chance to set a baseline for summer vacation days and longer vacations to make sure one partner can't suddenly demand to get more time during a summer or on holidays "just because." Certainly, exceptions to the rules can be made, but in any disagreement the written legal contract can easily be referenced and will prevail.

Random school holidays and shorter three day weekends will usually fall under the regular custody schedule routine, but could be divided up if special preferences are requested.

DISCUSS EVERYTHING

It is imperative to discuss how each parent is going to contribute financially to taking care of the child and how they will balance this with their work life. A key question to discuss is whether or not both parents will work. Depending on your answer, you can start to think about childcare expenses. For most people, childcare is not only expensive, but it comes with a host of pros and cons in terms of exposure to other kids, negligent or predatory caregivers, kids constantly getting sick, and more. If you're not interested in putting your child in childcare, you can discuss whether or not your extended families can help care for your child while both parents are working.

It's important to commit to the items you feel very strongly about within the legal document, like a child's health insurance and what type of education you want to provide for them. This includes not only primary and high school, but how you plan to fund their college education. If you want to contribute one amount until your child reaches a certain age and then change to a different figure later, this should be put into a legal document. It is hard to predict the future, but lean on your attorney for suggestions from documents they've prepared for others.

You'll also want to think about which parent will claim the child as their dependent for tax and reporting purposes. A parent who only makes a certain amount of money and claims the child as a dependent may get state or federal benefits. Under some circumstances, however, it might make more sense for the other partner to claim the child—for instance, if they have a more significant tax bill.

INSURE YOURSELF

People don't tend to think about how expensive medical care can be when you don't have insurance. Reality check: pregnancies are expensive, especially when they don't go according to plan.

Because she didn't have insurance, the medical procedures Anna went through following her ectopic pregnancy removal left her bankrupt and emotionally distraught.

Even with good health insurance, medical care for pre-screening, prenatal care, pregnancy, birth, and beyond can be a significant cost the two partners should discuss and budget for beforehand. An average pregnancy can cost between five and thirty thousand dollars,[74] depending on prenatal care and vaginal vs. cesarean birth.[75] To cover the cost of pregnancy and any potential complications, there needs to be health insurance in place or plenty of cash resources.

Health insurance is trickier for two people who aren't married. Insurance companies have created options for unmarried domestic partners now, but both people have to reside in the same home. It may take some creative problem-solving, but it's imperative that both parties are covered. Providing funding for health insurance can be included in your legal documents, but considering the ever rising costs and that it is often contingent on employment, I would advise to not put it in the legal documents as an absolute requirement, but instead list it in your Shared Expectations Document as a commitment.

POLICIES ARE CHANGING

As Parenting Partnerships are becoming more mainstream, the laws are beginning to catch up and are recognizing these partnerships legally. In Ontario, Canada, birth parents can sign a legal agreement to co-parent with up to four people, which allows potential spouses of Parenting Partners to have decision making power, if agreed upon.[76] California governor Jerry Brown passed a similar law in 2013, stating more than two people can legally be considered as parents and a recent ruling in the UK acknowledged that two people can be recognized as platonic parents.

Just remember, the point of the legal document isn't to be obsessive of every minor detail; nor include every item that you want to provide for your child. It's meant to be a guideline that both parties can live with and provide consistently. It is also an emergency dispute resolution tool, if a disagreement ever reaches that point.

The journey of raising a child comes with indescribable joy and innumerable rewards, but also plenty of challenges. Most of the challenges you'll have to figure out as you go along. So, it only makes sense to create watertight legal documents around the issues that you can anticipate.

CHAPTER 7

CREATING A SHARED EXPECTATIONS DOCUMENT

As opposed to the legal documents in the previous chapter, your Shared Expectations Document is not legally binding, but serves as the revered guide for interacting with your partner and prioritizing your child. Your Shared Expectations Document memorializes many of the things you *offer, want and expect* from yourself, from your Parenting Partner, and for your baby.

It also sets you on the right track, keeps you accountable and helps to navigate the inevitable disagreements that will arise in the future. It allows you to offer more to the partnership for the benefit of both your partner and child without being legally bound to provide those extra benefits for eighteen years. For

Anna and me, we always had the touchstone of our Shared Expectations Document to quickly get back in alignment.

DISCUSS AND OFFER WHAT YOU CAN

When people decide to have a baby, their lives suddenly become opened up to a million unexpected things—mental health issues like postpartum depression are quite common. What if one of the partners loses their job and you fall into sudden financial challenges? You could lose your healthcare benefits and insurance. You might give birth to a child with special needs, developmental difficulties, or serious health issues. The bottom line is, bringing a child into the world comes with a high degree of uncertainty. These possibilities need to be discussed and where applicable, documented before conception. While you can't write down everything, if you have the major foundational issues and the common items addressed, it allows you to focus more clearly on the unexpected.

Even when a baby is born healthy, it should follow that everything after that is just icing on the cake, right? Well, 98% yes, but there is a lot to the remaining 2%. A healthy, happy baby is a tremendous blessing and something for which to be incredibly grateful. However, raising a child can put stress on even the healthiest of adults because the stakes are so high. Every decision, from what type of baby food and diapers to buy, to whether a high fever requires a doctor visit, can have a big impact on the little person you are just getting to know.

It's quite common for even the highest functioning parents to experience conflict around how they raise children. I believe this is largely because of the complexity of each parent's past experiences, expectations for their child and their vision of ideal parents. Since these items are so detailed and nuanced they *cannot be fully disclosed and discussed before* embarking on the journey of parenthood. Most romantic partners who are considering having a child don't spend copious amounts of time setting expectations about vacations, careers, living arrangements and household responsibilities. To note, some married couples get divorced because they never even had a serious discussion on whether they did or didn't want to have children — unbelievable but true. A significant advantage of Parenting Partnerships is that the intentional nature of the arrangement creates a natural opening for parents to have these "parental expectations" conversations well ahead of time.

A big part of my insistence on setting shared expectations stems from my own parents' marital difficulties and prolonged separation. Two years of constant, aggressive in-house fighting led to another two years of very rigid separation. The four years when I was eleven to fourteen-years-old were extremely difficult. I felt the pain and shame of being shuffled back and forth between households and spending every other weekend three hours away with my father. I knew I didn't want to raise a child in an environment of hot acrimony and icy separation. I dealt with mixed messages from two separate households with two completely different sets of beliefs, viewpoints and rules, with no consistency between the two parenting styles and little-to-no positive communication between my parents.

For that reason, when I said yes to Anna it was far from a simple or straightforward "yes." Instead, it was a yes loaded with ideas, considerations, conditions and expectations. I asked for ten specific things that would set boundaries, meet my preconceived needs in parenthood, and help align our expectations about child-rearing. Our goal was simple, we wanted to do everything in our power to create healthy expectations to lead to a healthy environment that met both our thresholds for proper parenting. We had to have alignment on major issues, and mechanisms to avoid major disagreements. All of this had to be done up front, *before* we had a child. If Anna and I hadn't discussed and agreed upon the following expectations, I would not have moved forward, or if we had, then our partnership would not have gone so smoothly and may have failed altogether.

THE LIST

I. MARRIAGE

First, I wanted to clarify that Anna and I were planning a Parenting Partnership with the same goal in mind and with no hidden agendas. I was straightforward about the fact that we would not be getting married—ever. This was a non-negotiable for me. We were exes for a reason and no matter the gravitational pull of being parents, we were not going to get married.

Anna agreed with me and understood. A significant amount of time had passed since we'd been romantically involved with each other, and we hadn't even seen each other for over a year and a half. We'd both gone on to date other people, and any residual romantic feelings were long gone. I wanted to make sure we both intended to keep it that way.

Agreement on this issue was particularly important given that we would be conceiving our baby the "natural" way. For Parenting Partners choosing to have a baby through intercourse, it's crucial to establish a period of monogamy or abstinence during the pregnancy, because other sexual relationships could pose a health risk to the baby. It's also important not to mistake sexual fidelity and intercourse for conception as anything romantic.

I'm sure from time to time among all the Parenting Partnerships in the world, some partners do decide to get married. However, going into a Parenting Partnership hoping that a romance will blossom between yourself and your partner is a recipe for disaster—along with being dastardly manipulative. Much like having a baby to save a marriage, it doesn't work. Anna and I went into the partnership agreeing that the marriage door was closed.

2. RELIGIOUS UPBRINGING

It's important for both partners to consider how their child will be raised in relation to a specific faith. Spiritual beliefs and practices can form an important part of a child's identity and provide consistency in their life. They also can affect educational choices, like choosing a daycare or school with a certain religious affiliation.

Religion also plays a role in how you organize your schedule and social engagements. What holidays you will celebrate? With what community will you surround yourself? Religion can also form an important bond between the child, the parents, and extended family, especially in mid childhood. It can set a framework for connections that dictate interactions and moral social structure through adulthood.

Anna and I had a fairly easy situation to resolve, as she was raised Catholic and I was raised Protestant. Although not exactly the same, they're likely easier to reconcile than a fully cross-cultural combination of faiths or ideologies would have been. My strong preference was for the child to be raised Protestant, as I take issues with many aspects of Catholicism. Anna was willing to agree on this expectation.

For some Parenting Partners, discussing religion early in the decision-making process is important—ideally it's good to discuss many times, because it's one of the areas where otherwise agreeable partners may not be able to reach a compromise. That's not to say it's impossible for two completely different religious views to find a compromise that lets each of them honor their individual beliefs with their child.

The key to reaching this accord, however, is getting comfortable with compromise ahead of time. It isn't fair to your child, or your Parenting Partner, to suddenly become more rigorous about religious upbringing years down the road.

3. NAMING THE BABY

Names carry deep personal, cultural and familial connections. Research has shown that first and last names can affect personalities and outcomes for a child.[77,78] I felt if the child didn't have my last name, it could seem like I wasn't truly involved; it might feel as though the baby was Anna's more than mine. Furthermore, sharing a name would punctuate my commitment as the father. I wanted the world to know this was my child.

For me, I wanted there to be a sense of normalcy for our child. In an already unconventional situation, it seemed wise to have one less thing setting our child apart from other kids. With two involved parents and a last name the same as the father's, the child might be less inclined to feel different from their friends. As an added bonus, outsiders might be less inclined to ask intrusive questions that might make the child uncomfortable. That being said, Robert's last name is different from his mother's, but in today's day and age many women are choosing to retain their maiden names so we have had only one to two questions regarding the difference.

4. INVOLVED PARENTING

For me, becoming a father meant being deeply involved in my child's life, including being present for a combination of daily or weekly interactions and larger events. I wanted to be there for school pick-ups and drop-offs, after school activities, chaperoning field trips and for great summer vacations and family holiday celebrations. This was essential for me.

I envisioned myself seeing my child multiple times a week, or more. The typical "divorced parent" custody schedule is generally every other weekend, with a couple of hours on a weekday night. That limited, spaced out time allotment wasn't enough for me to agree to become a dad.

Lessons I wanted to teach my child need to be passed on through almost daily interaction. I believe the way to nurture a relationship with anyone is through a series of smaller, sweet engagements. I knew that if I saw my child multiple times per week, I'd be able to build trust, reinforce how much I loved and cared about them, and show that I'd always be there for them. Joint custody was my strong expectation. I wanted my voice to be heard on all educational or health-related matters and attend all parent-teacher conferences and doctor visits. I also wanted to be available to attend sporting events and extra-curricular activities. If a teacher was looking for parent volunteers I wanted to be asked to participate because I was the child's father.

Even on the days I was not with my child, I expected either of us to have open communication access. We would not bicker over phone calls during each other's time. When I wasn't with my child, I wanted to be able to video chat with them and receive photo updates from daily life that I could share with my family and friends. I was more than willing to offer this same access to Anna during my designated times so we could both feel present even if we were not physically there.

The most highly involved parents still can't predict the future. While general custody arrangements and time designations need to be outlined in your legal documents *before* entering into any sort of Parenting Partnership, both parties should be prepared to readjust your Shared Expectations Document if future events require a significant schedule change to the agreed upon expectations.

If both parents are as committed and eager as they should be, the hard part won't be convincing someone to honor their legal custody requirements, but instead it will be finding enough time each week for each parent. Also, coming to equitable time allotment for holidays, special occasions, and memorable moments. In my Parenting Partnerships we sometimes celebrate holidays together, sometimes apart, and sometimes we have multiple celebrations so both parents get to show their love and share their families.

Some parents are adamant about being the main caregiver in sickness, or having kids participate in sports, or taking the same two weeks at the same summer vacation spot every year. These parental passions should be celebrated, accommodated and used to provide the child with the best possible upbringing.

What would be very hard to accommodate would be an inflexible, time consuming, individual passion that consistently doesn't allow for flexibility in scheduling. These can manifest in a variety of seemingly healthy ways; avid hikers, golf addicts, theater enthusiasts, triathletes, chess wizards. Other less obvious ways, but still difficult to justify with parental responsibilities may be incessantly volunteering or working extra hours at a job they love but that pays minimally. This will impact that partner's schedule and, in turn, impact the other partner, while not offering much in the way of additional benefits for the child. While Parenting Partnership offers more time for these types of pursuits than a marriage might, you still have to curb them to fulfill your new role in a Parenting Partnership.

5. FAMILY INTEGRATION

Beyond my personal time with our little one, I was going to need flexibility of schedule and vacations to fully integrate the little one into my immediate and extended family, with whom I am very close. It was vital that Anna understand how important this was to me as she has a much smaller family that is not as close. A dynamic, large, close family like mine can be overwhelming for those who didn't grow up in one.

This is another area where Parenting Partnerships differ from a conventional married-with-kids situation. Parenting Partners are not required to interact with in-laws or attend the other partner's family events which can often be a negative in a marriage. Anna chooses to attend occasionally and at her and my discretion. Most importantly I set the expectation that she would need to be flexible for birthdays, anniversaries, weddings, holidays and family reunions, which requires significant scheduling. As mentioned previously, I wanted my child to be accessible via video chat to my immediate family as well which was a big ask, but it really reinforced a positive, inclusive environment for Robert.

6. GEOGRAPHIC PROXIMITY

A non-negotiable condition of my having a child with Anna was that we must live in the same city. The last thing I was willing to accept was being a thousand miles away from my child. Anna understood this was one of my greatest fears and biggest risks. If I'd asked her to live near me but she questioned the necessity of my request, that would have been a huge red flag. Clearly, both parents need to value being within a short commute so both parents can develop a healthy relationship with the child. The closer, the better. The same street or next door is not out of the question. Ideally, both partners will live in a city where they have family and connection to community. It's much easier to grow into the parenting role in a place where you are comfortable and have a network of support.

At the time Anna and I were discussing this potential partnership she was living with her parents in Michigan and I was in Texas. We agreed that Anna and the baby would live with her parents to have her family's caregiving support and be financially responsible. We appreciated and were humbled by the massive support her family had given during her medical struggles and the potentially vulnerable pregnancy. I promised to spend as much time in Michigan as possible and actually spent ninety-four days (26%) of the first year there caring for Robert. We agreed that after two years she would move south to wherever I was living at that time for work. We later revisited this decision and agreed to have them in Michigan a little longer with them ultimately moving to Texas when Robert was two-and-a-half.

Those first two years were quite tough on the two of us, financially and emotionally as they are on almost all new parents. My biggest regret was, that by being in different locations, I ended up missing Robert's birth by a few hours as he arrived one week early even though the doctor assured us that there was no way Anna would give birth that weekend. Argh! Admittedly, Robert arrived so unexpectedly and was delivered so quickly that even Anna's family members who lived in town missed his arrival. I showed up a few hours late.

While it was simply unlucky timing, I will always regret the fact that I wasn't present for my son's birth. For this reason, I strongly recommend both parties live in proximity to one another starting with conception and no later than a few months before the due date. This proximity will also allow for more bonding interactions during the pregnancy.

7. FINANCIAL SUPPORT

The basic financial components I was willing to offer as a father were included in the legal documents and would be routed through the state's child support mechanism. The additional financial extras items that I wanted to provide to my child would be provided directly as would any additional contributions I was going to make to Anna.

How much should one Parenting Partner expect the other to contribute to throwing a birthday party? Which parent should fund a child's holiday gifts to friends and relatives? At what age will your child be allowed to have a phone or a computer or a car and who will be responsible to pay for these things?

Two partners will likely agree on the majority of basic items when it comes to raising a child—such as groceries, education, medical care, insurance, and school supplies. These are the types of expenses that child support is meant to cover. Clothing, strollers, transportation, and housing get more difficult because they are more expensive and personal preferences start to seep into your expectations. We had long discussions on the standard of clothing, vehicles and housing (this includes the neighborhood) we'd like to uphold for our child.

But as any parent can tell you, there are plenty of expenses beyond those basics that go into raising a child. Other expenses that the partners should discuss include extracurricular activities, summer camps, allowance, travel, etc. Anna let me know her thoughts and I shared mine. Setting expectations about how much additional financial support each partner will provide beyond the basic court-ordered amount takes significant planning. Obviously, the amount depends on one's financial discipline and ability to pay so be realistic if not a bit conservative. Under-promise, over-deliver!

With Anna's plan to stay with family for a couple more years and then move down south to join me, I was willing to contribute more money so she could extend her stay-at-home period through the infant and toddler phases. Supporting Anna financially so she could be a stay-at-home mom for a few years instead of a few months is something we both worked hard to achieve. We knew it would be a financial hit for both of us, but we wanted our child to have a similar stay-at-home mom situation as we both did as kids with our married mom households. Seeing as she was willing to live with her parents and take time off from career at thirty-one and I had attained a certain level of financial stability at thirty-five, we felt confident we could make this expectation a reality.

The vast majority of Parenting Partnerships, just like married households, will have two working parents and will need to have a serious discussion about the viability of a parent staying at home for an extended period, if at all. This may not be an option or a desire depending on the details of your partnership. No matter your financial situation, it needs to be clearly and explicitly communicated. Money disputes can derail any type of relationship, so you have to do your best to avoid surprises. In my experience, making and documenting financial arrangements ahead of time is one of the major advantages Parenting Partnerships offer over traditional marriages.

8. TOTAL COMMITMENT TO ESTABLISHING A HEALTHY, LOVING ENVIRONMENT

Anna and I were going into the Parenting Partnership with two dreams. First—high above all others—we hoped, prayed and dreamt to have a healthy baby. Second, we wanted to create a healthy environment around that child, and love and nurture him. When challenges arose, we both agreed to ask ourselves what a great parent would do—and then do exactly that.

It was really important to me that, if I chose to become a father, I would gladly make whatever sacrifices and compromises necessary to raise a healthy, happy child. Questioning whether I had it in me to properly love and care for a child also led me to think carefully about Anna's capacity to do the same. If we weren't on the same page about stepping up and into our fullest potential as parents, then we shouldn't enter into a Parenting Partnership. Wanting a child was one thing, but we had to be sure that we were truly in a place to commit and make that child the highest priority and joy in life.

To that end, Anna and I discussed what a great parent looked like to each of us. Anna's version of a devoted parent is one who makes raising their child the top purpose in life. I could not have agreed more. Essentially, we set the shared expectation that no other priority—work, love, self—would come before Robert. We would devote as much time and effort as was necessary to constantly surround him with a healthy emotional environment in which to grow.

9. LIFESTYLE PREFERENCES

At the time Anna asked me to father a child, my life was very full of professional and social activities that were likely to impact our relationship as Parenting Partners. I needed Anna to agree that she wouldn't expect to dictate what I did, professionally or socially, or make me feel guilty about any decisions I made that didn't directly affect our child. I would extend this same courtesy to her.

While I knew I would have a multitude of obligations to be a good parent, this wasn't a marriage and neither of us would have to sign over 100% of our personal independence. I certainly agreed that my professional and social life would come second to our child's best interests, but outside of parenting, Anna and I would respect each other's freedom.

This is another huge benefit of Parenting Partnerships. Each person has time to live their own lives, with this individuality being respected. There's no dictating that either of us has to significantly change our approach to life to the preferences of the other parent. The fact that we're having a child is going to require that we do things differently in order to fulfill our parental responsibilities, but there is freedom in how we parent and how we live. While we may not always love the other parent's social or professional choices, I chose to have this child with this person. I chose them because I believe they are fundamentally mature, responsible and caring. If I didn't believe those things, I never would have entered into this partnership. If they're a mature responsible adult, then you need to trust and respect their lifestyle as long as it is not illegal, destructive or directly detrimental to your child.

10. OTHER PARENTING PARTNERS

As I mentioned earlier, I came to the realization that it was possible I may never feel the need to get married or have more children if I had a child through a Parenting Partnership.

However, I knew I'd have roughly another thirty years of being able to father children. If becoming a parent brought me the joy I expected, would I want to become a father for a second or third time?

To me, keeping my parenting options open seemed like a reasonable request, much like continuing to date and have a social life while being a Parenting Partner. Moreover, in my personal assessments I identified a desire to have multiple children and didn't want my child to be an only child. Having siblings had been a great joy in my life, and I anticipated wanting the same for my child.

If the opportunity for me to become a father a second time as a Parenting Partner or husband should arise in the future, I wanted the option to pursue it. So, it was necessary to establish this expectation with Anna at the outset. I simply told her "if I do this with you, I may do this with someone else." As it turns out this was prescient twofold.

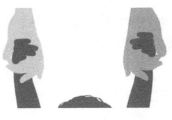

CHAPTER 8

THINGS WE WISH WE'D DISCUSSED OR DONE

At this point the main concepts of this book have been laid out and you may be thinking, "This is pretty straightforward, manageable and potentially something that could work for me. This guy seems really upbeat about his Parenting Partnership experiences, so what is the catch and where is the drama?" If so, you are exactly where you should be and drawing the proper positive conclusions. Spoiler alert, none of that positivity will change between now and the end of the book. Have fun reading on without looking for any huge negatives!

The list of ten items from the previous chapter is a great start, and they certainly took a long time to talk through, but it is just the tip of the proverbial Parenting Partner discussion iceberg. Anna and I spent months (and to a lesser degree

Sophia and I since it was my second time through) discussing and agreeing on all these issues before our child was born. In retrospect, there are a few things that I wish we'd discussed in more detail and some things we should have done before launching our Parenting Partnership.

TIME AT HOME THEN BACK TO WORK

Post pregnancy bonding is no doubt very important.[79] Anna and I felt strongly that she should stay at home as long as possible to focus 100% of her time on Robert. We had this in our Shared Expectations Document as described earlier, but what we didn't have were clear milestones for the ending of this arrangement.

It quickly became apparent that being a stay-at-home mom suited Anna and she was reluctant to change this enhanced arrangement even years later as Robert became much easier to manage as a toddler and a preschooler. While there was certainly still a lot of work to be done, it was not the best use of her time and talents. As we were both first time parents, we didn't know the schedule or anticipate the extra free time she would have once Robert started preK classes and early elementary school. Her desire to continue being a stay at home mom started to cause friction as I had assumed (incorrectly) that she would desire to return to work as soon as possible.

Every year a child gets older, they become more involved with school, friends, and extracurricular activities. This leaves a stay-at-home partner with more time to pursue personal activities, especially if they have a network of friends who can help with pick-ups and drop-offs. These extra available hours can be put towards learning new skills, part-time or gig work outside of the house, or work-from-home opportunities.

Not only does part-time work bring additional financial resources to the partnership which can reduce stress, lower the financial burden on the earning partner and create an opportunity for savings, but it can also help the formerly stay-at-home partner to reintegrate themselves into the workforce in anticipation of the day when the other partner's financial support will end. Jobs such as real estate agent or ride-share driver are just a couple of the income producing opportunities for partners who have limited hours available while staying at home during a child's formative years. Anna was not idle as she kept very busy with Robert and some online reselling as a home-based business which brought in "coffee and workout money," but didn't move the needle financially or prepare her for the next phase of her career. Looking back, our Shared Expectations Document should have better stipulated when the stay-at-home partner would get back to work and the contributing partner no longer have to provide the enhanced post-pregnancy contributions. Using milestones such as a child's age or grade would have saved some tough conversations about when career-focused work would resume and certain extra finances end.

'IT WAS ON SALE' VERSUS 'DO WE NEED IT'

Child products run the gamut and all of them market themselves to seem necessary. As a Parenting Partner, I'm contributing funds for everyday life. I'm giving money toward my child's well-being. Along these same lines, I also wish we'd had a more explicit conversation about what each party thinks are reasonable expenses. For example, what is an appropriate amount to spend on kids shoes or a child's haircut? Anna and I had differing opinions on the specifics of what was needed for clothing. While these everyday expenses seem minor, a discrepancy of opinion can cause arguments and financial stress. Sounds just like your friend's or family member's marriage? On these topics it certainly does.

FAMILY CONNECTIONS AND RESOURCES

Because you aren't married and don't have long conversations with your Parenting Partner daily, you may be unaware of special connections and resources to which your partner has access. For example, my second Parenting Partner's (Sophia) aunt worked at a Montessori school and we were able to get hugely discounted access to early education. Her sister managed a dessert store and got a 50% discount. Anna's father was an excellent carpenter who fixed up anything and everything when they would come to visit. These are connections that married couples take for granted, but need to be ferreted out by Parenting Partners for the benefit of all involved. Also discuss the level of caretaking involvement from each family. Both Parenting Partners and my boys benefited from living with extended family at different times. The different family units were able to offer extra care (cooking, cleaning, transportation) and babysitting to alleviate childcare issues at no cost with the added benefit of integration and creating a healthy, nurturing environment.

OUTSIDE OPINIONS

In retrospect, we should have discussed our policies for handling criticism, either from family members or the outside world. This turned out to be a bigger challenge than either of us anticipated because Anna and I handled this pressure differently. This is more complicated than it seems. You need a plan. You need to emotionally prepare. You also need to explain to outsiders what a Parenting Partnership is, how it works, and why you chose to have a child this way.

The more logically and succinctly you can guide your family and friends through this rationale the better. Readers of this book will have a great advantage; they can give a copy of the book to skeptical friends and family and ask them to read certain passages. Anna and I didn't have that luxury. We will address this further in chapter ten.

ADDITIONAL CHILDREN

It was known to me, and I did mention it, but I likely should have been even more direct and documented it better, that I was only willing to have one child with each of my Parenting Partners. Having multiple children within a Parenting

Partnership is of course a possibility, and a logical argument for it can easily be made as you have already established the ground rules, infrastructure and the children would be full siblings, but I personally would not have been comfortable with that arrangement. Conversely, I was very interested in exploring adopting a child or fostering children in concert with my Parenting Partners. Unfortunately, when presented to Anna and Sophia neither of them showed much interest in opening their homes which saddens me, as it feels like a lost opportunity. At one point one of my Parenting Partners approached me to have another child, which I declined when offered.

Additionally, I received two other serious inquiries from women that were genuinely interested in entering into a Parenting Partnership; one was a lesbian, former-employee and the other an over-forty friend from school. While flattered, I declined for multiple personal reasons, mostly that I was not interested in having more than two Parenting Partnerships. Seeing as it is an interesting and unique story being retold often, I still get many half-serious inquiries regarding availability.

Experienced parent note: taking care of one young child is a breeze all things considered. Taking care of two young children is not a doubling of the effort, but closer to a tripling or a quadrupling. Three or more children of similar age really is all consuming.

When Sophia was engaged, her fiance had a daughter who did interact with Anthony and it was their plan to have additional children of their own. Conversations about how this would affect our dynamic did start and went fairly well, but ultimately didn't progress too far as the engagement ended.

With prolific breeders such as Elon Musk, Nick Cannon, The Duggars and Octomom, it is important to ask your potential partner how many children they hope to have and why. If the answer is "nineteen and counting" then that may be a deal breaker.

FUTURE ROMANTIC INTERESTS INTERACTING WITH YOUR CHILD

Robust discussion—opinions, attitudes, concerns, worst-case scenarios—should occur around each partner's take on when, how and where future romantic interests of either partner would interact with your child. While casual dating falls under Chapter Seven, point #9 Lifestyle Preferences (in that dating activities are none of each other's business), if you or your partner enters into a serious dating relationship that will likely precipitate two meetings: one with the other partner and one with the child. Even though this may never happen and likely won't happen in the near future, it really deserves more attention than I gave it during my discussions with either Anna or Sophia. While our two Parenting Partnerships have successfully navigated through my dating, engagement and marriage to Natalie and a serious relationship with a short engagement by Sophia, everyone would have benefited from better expectation setting on this topic.

What relationship milestones would need to be achieved for both of you to feel comfortable with a romantic interest being introduced to your child? How would that introduction be handled? What additional milestones would have to be reached for romantic sleepovers if the child is on premises? How do things change when the milestones of engagement and marriage are achieved? Parenting Partnerships are somewhat complex already and future romantic partners for the participants certainly add new complexity. Basically, assume it is going to happen for each of the partners and discuss how that would play out. And then memorialize those agreements into your expectation setting document!!

THINGS WE WISH WE HAD DONE

Much has changed since 2005 and even over the years of planning, writing and researching this book. The availability and affordability of genetic testing along with advances in fertility testing give Parenting Partners an opportunity to increase the odds of a healthy pregnancy. The following are a few actions that you should take as you progress along the path to a Parenting Partnership:

- Get fertility tests on each partner done prior to conception attempts and before you are too far into your document creation. Otherwise, you both may end up doing a lot of planning and legal work up front without ever actually conceiving a child. Men can pretty easily get a sperm mobility, motility, and count test with a fertility specialist to determine sperm viability. It's rare for a sample not to have any viable sperm, but it's worth checking. Women should begin tracking ovulation. If any irregularities are noted, they should see a fertility specialist immediately for diagnostics. Some tests include transvaginal ultrasound, hysteroscopy, or hysterosalpingogram (HSG) test. These tests can range in price from $500-$3000.[80, 81]

Preconception genetic testing with expanded carrier screening (ECS), and/or preimplantation genetic testing for polygenic disorders (PGT-P) are smart options to ensure both partners are not carriers of certain genetic abnormalities that could result in a tragic situation for the child.[82] When you're going into this situation with your eyes open in every other regard, it's worth being 100% sure that you and your partner have the highest odds of having a healthy baby. If not, what does this mean for your conception planning? What is your risk tolerance? What expenses may be necessary?

If conceiving naturally, both parents absolutely need to get STD testing done before conception efforts to be certain of your sexual health status. Having this test will set expectations in a positive way, prevent insecurities, and avoid negativity. Past and present STDs can significantly inhibit your ability to conceive. It also serves as a safeguard against any STD that could be harmful to the baby.[83] Along these same lines, if you are conceiving naturally, partners very likely need to abstain from any sexual involvement with others. Sexual activity outside of the proposed Parenting Partnership adds a lot of complexity and risk.

Another significant change since my partnerships started in 2006 and 2010 is the ubiquitousness of social media. I've never been a fan and neither were Anna or Sophia, but many people are. Two topics to discuss: first, agreeing on what information, if any, will be shared publicly about the early phases of your Parenting Partner journey and second, share with your partner your feelings about posting pictures of your child on social networks. Many parents are now choosing not to post their children's faces on the internet. These preferences would need to be communicated to family and friends.

THIS ISN'T A NEGOTIATION AND DON'T MAKE IT ONE

An important point I want to make is that discussing expectations with your partner may sound like a negotiation, but it's really not. Try not to think of it that way. You really don't want it to be a negotiation. Some people are talented negotiators and some are not. A sharp negotiator will have a distinct advantage and may "win" in the short term by getting their way. But after the dust settles, resentment may build in the other partner if they feel they have been taken advantage of. Or the "sharp negotiator" may be frustrated because the other partner is incapable of fulfilling what was agreed upon. It's better to think of this as a mutual discussion of what both partners feel they need and what they can offer, and then searching for common ground.

It's easy to say "yes" to a request in the abstract. If one person says they want to have all the holidays and you don't really celebrate holidays or have an extended family and you like to work holidays to get double pay, you may give them up. Then you find yourself alone and sad on those days wishing you could spend time with your child. To properly assess these possible concessions, you need to dig deeper into the details of your unique situation. Think through how the proposed experience will feel and what it will look like and how that will play out in reality. Obviously, some considerations have more weight than others. Seeing your child specifically on a calendar date isn't as important as your level of parental involvement or being genuinely devoted to raising that child, but it still may matter more than you initially think.

If you simply cannot agree with your prospective Parenting Partner on some of the most important topics, I'd suggest putting everything on pause or just calling it off. I can't imagine two partners moving forward successfully if they fail to agree on a number of crucial considerations.

THE FOUNDATION FOR SUCCESS

Setting proper expectations pours a foundation of success in any type of partnership. Consider the statistic that couples who participate in premarital counseling report higher levels of marital satisfaction and experience and a 30% decline in divorce.[84] This higher success rate is because the couple took the time to candidly discuss expectations *before* getting married. As a result, some states are looking to make premarital counseling a requirement. It's an excellent idea to seek professional counseling before entering a Parenting Partnership.

Professional counseling sessions can reveal a lot about the other person, and yourself. However, even with these revelations, people don't always set expectations ahead of time because they want to avoid disagreements. It can be hard to have the courage to communicate openly and honestly before you enter into a partnership, but getting introspective, significant, and accurate answers beforehand is essential.

Today there are innumerable articles, books, and resources available to assist in opening communication about the topics with which new parents struggle. Unfortunately, when it comes to forming Parenting Partnerships, the advice and resources aren't quite as widespread. With this book I hope, in part, to rectify that.

In the situation Anna and I faced, our recognition of the unpaved path we were pursuing drove us to go the extra mile in getting prepared. Even with this preparation, we did not do counseling before conception, and I wish we had. We ultimately sought counseling during our Parenting Partnership to make communication flow even more easily, but likely would have benefited greatly from preconception counseling.

CONFLICT RESOLUTION

Since there is no way to predict every conceivable conflict that might arise years down the road, there should also be a conflict resolution process agreed to in advance. There is a conflict resolution system within the legal system, but once you get a lawyer and go to court, it's almost never a positive experience.

Within this document of shared expectations, it's advantageous to establish a group of respected family members or friends, whom you both trust, that you can use as mediators if necessary. The people you choose should be supportive of your Parenting Partnership and want to advise with love and respect in the best interest of your child and partnership. When things become difficult, you both can sit down with these people before the argument escalates into something unmanageable or goes in front of the court.

Beyond the document, ask questions about how your partner likes to communicate about difficult topics—email, phone, text, in-person, within a group? Do they have an environment that is most preferred for them—office, home, park, a coffee shop? What time of day is typically best? What day of the week? Of course some matters may be urgent, but do your best to respect boundaries and preferences in order to quickly and effectively problem solve.

At this point the list may seem exhaustive, but we did not even cover specific approaches to education, politics, discipline or a multitude of other topics that a Parenting Partner may be passionate about. Wild, real-life example: a married, professional linguist chose to only speak to his newborn son in the fictional language of Klingon from the Star Trek series for the first three years of the child's life.[85] Pretty bizarre. Human beings are an amazingly diverse group so don't be afraid to ask anything and make sure you are sharing anything and everything you can think of about your childhood experiences, hopes, wants and dreams to improve your chance of having a great Parenting Partnership experience!!

CHAPTER 9

ANNA'S EXPERIENCE

Up until this point in the book you've heard me make my case for why Parenting Partnerships are an attractive and viable option for people who want to have, share and prioritize a child but aren't in a committed relationship or a marriage. You know how I feel about Parenting Partnerships, but how do my Parenting Partners feel about the idea? Are they as happy and satisfied with the arrangement as I am? Is it as fulfilling for them as it is for me?

In this chapter I present an interview with Anna. I think there is tremendous value in hearing her thoughts on the topic. As you'll see, we do not agree on everything, but on the big things we are well-aligned; and that's what's important for our child.

Anna is the definition of an involved mom, volunteering for everything at Robert's school from chaperoning field trips to soliciting serious donations for school fundraisers. The other moms love her for this, her accent and her sharp sense of humor. She has a close social circle of married friends with whom she enjoys spending most of her free time.

Anna's answers have been edited slightly for length and clarity, but the meaning is exactly as she intended and with her approval. There is a bit of repetition of what I've written about earlier in the book, but I think it's important to hear her perspective on these events.

Anna's interview begins here.

MY MEDICAL ISSUES

Q: This Parenting Partnership began when you were experiencing a serious medical issue, can you elaborate?

I went through an unpleasant couple of years before Robert was conceived, so unpleasant that I erased a lot of those experiences from my memory. The basics are that I was twenty-eight-years-old and, after visiting Frank in Chicago and sleeping with him for the last time, I began experiencing deep physical pain. I had dealt with endometriosis for years, but this was far more severe than anything I'd felt before.

When I went to the hospital, they asked me if I was pregnant. I said I wasn't, but the doctors did a pregnancy test anyway. It revealed I was pregnant—the first shock. Then, we did an ultrasound which showed that the fetus was not positioned in the right place, hence my pain.

The baby wasn't going to survive—it didn't even have a pulse—so the doctors terminated the pregnancy. In the process, my fallopian tube, ovary, and cervix all got damaged. Around that time, after more testing, it was discovered that there were cancerous cells in my cervix.

In early November, and again right before the holidays, I underwent the first two of four scraping treatments to remove the cancer cells from my cervix. Everything seemed fine, but I learned that I would likely have trouble carrying to a full-term pregnancy because the treatments had left my cervix so thin.

By the time I turned twenty-nine, the cancer cells had come back three more times, requiring more scraping treatments. According to the doctors, if I experienced the problem one more time, there would be no chance for me to ever carry a child.

Q: How did that affect you emotionally and physically?

Emotionally, I was devastated. Financially I was devastated. One of my biggest dreams has always been to be a parent, and I always thought I'd be a fantastic mother. For me, it was horrible to want something so badly, only to have a doctor say it most likely won't ever happen.

I started taking medications and hormones in an attempt to fix the situation. In a way, this was successful. The doctors and I determined I *was* able to get pregnant, as my one healthy ovary was producing eggs every other month! However, because of my endometriosis, I would have difficulty holding the pregnancy.

With the triple threat of ectopic pregnancy, endometriosis, and cancer cells, the doctors told me I had only a 15% chance of having a child within a very narrow window of time—once I came off the hormones. I'd only have three opportunities in the next six months to conceive a child.

MY SPECIAL REQUEST TO FRANK

Q: What happened next?

I called Frank the following summer and told him that I had six months to try and have a child. I asked him how he felt about becoming the father of my child. It had been a year since I'd seen Frank, but I knew he was living his own, very separate life in Houston.

I remember sitting in my car, talking him through all the percentages, and finally asking him if he was in or if he was out. I was trying to sell the idea to him in any way I could. I knew Frank and I got along well, and I thought parenting together would be a positive experience. Frank had told me he'd always wanted to have a child, and I suggested that this would be a good opportunity for him to get what he wanted.

He didn't agree immediately and suggested I consider other options. After he'd thought about it, though, he said there was a possibility that we could move forward. He thought I'd be an excellent mom, and he saw potential for the partnership to work. However, he indicated he was going to compile a list of items which we needed to agree on before conceiving a child.

PUTTING THINGS IN WRITING

Q: What did you think about Frank's requirement that you have a solid agreement in place?

Frank and I were both 100% committed to raising a child and everything that came along with that journey. We were two individuals living in different states, but we knew we could make it work.

Frank and I have a custody arrangement, a legal document filed first with the state of Michigan and then with the state of Texas—that sets the amount of dollars sent on a monthly basis for child support. It also details when I have our son Robert and when Frank has him for both visitation and holidays.

The other parameters that Frank asked for were not negative for me in any way, shape or form and would not stop me from fulfilling my dream of having my own child.

Q: Have there been any challenges to that agreement?

Never have we had to enforce our custody agreement. We've always been good at working out when we'd each see Robert. Because Frank and I were great friends from the beginning and are still friends today, we've never had to use the legal agreement to prove anything.

Don't get me wrong—Frank and I had a few fights and have gone through some challenging times. Our legal document, however, was always only a backstop; that's why I'd definitely recommend for all Parenting Partners to create a similar legal document. It's comforting to know it's there, and it keeps us focused on the bigger picture of what's most important for our child.

Q: How does financial support work?

Our financial situation meant I didn't have to work for the early years and got to spend every day being a full-time mom. I dedicate all of my efforts toward Robert—which, in my opinion, is one of the reasons why he's such a great kid! We've never used childcare because one of us is always with him, either taking him to school or picking him up.

I'm grateful to Frank and my family for providing my household and my entire lifestyle, and I believe a relationship is much stronger when you don't have to worry or argue about money. I appreciate everything he does for me; my house is always open to him, and his is open to me.

REENTERING THE WORKFORCE

Q: What happens when the financial support ends?

I never stress about the situation between myself, Frank and Robert, but I do feel like Robert is growing up so fast. Then again, most mothers probably think this about their children. Time is flying by. When Robert turns eighteen in October 2024, our situation as Parenting Partners is going to change dramatically.

Right now, I'm not scared about what I'll do after Robert turns eighteen because I have been re-establishing my financial independence for many years now. Still, I haven't been back to a formal office or corporate environment for the past sixteen years. Over the next two years I will keep working and saving while still enjoying my last full years with Robert at home. What I'll do after that I am not 100% sure.

THE NEED FOR A SUPPORT SYSTEM

Q: How did your family react to the idea of a Parenting Partnership?

Family members can have different understandings or points of view on life. Some are bound to be more accepting than others, and some take time to understand the decision to enter a Parenting Partnership. On the whole, however, I'd say that I've been 100% supported by both my immediate and extended family.

Once I told them about the partnership with Frank, I had substantial support from my parents and my sister. My parents know how hard headed and strong-willed I am, they know that I won't take no for an answer.

My dad always envisioned that his daughter would follow the traditional path; he thought I would get married and then start a family. I told him that probably wasn't going to happen due to my medical condition. Once he understood, he was more than supportive of my decision. My sister is seven years younger than I am, but I remember her being supportive as well.

My mom came to many doctor appointments with me. Once, when I went outside and teared up, she knew something was wrong. I told her I wouldn't be able to carry a child, so if I ever did get pregnant, I would miscarry. Her response? "Anna, nobody ever tells you no." I couldn't agree more. My mindset was that I was going to have my own biological child, whatever it took.

Throughout the latter parts of the pregnancy, my family was there for me every step of the way. When I went into early labor, they drove me to the hospital. Once they met their grandson, they had no choice but to love him with all their hearts. They remain supportive to this day, and they agree that a Parenting Partnership with Frank was the best decision for me.

I've never sensed anything negative toward me, my decisions, or Robert. My sister now has a couple of kids who are amazing with Robert. All the cousins in my sister's husband's family know Robert and buy gifts for him, nobody is excluded. We're all one big, happy family.

As for Frank's family, we were extremely close for many years. In fact, Frank's sister and her family lived with me for a few months when they were moving to Texas from California while looking for a new home. But as Robert has gotten older and Frank got married I have seen the extended family less often. On the other hand, I now see Robert's little brothers and Natalie a few times a month and occasionally host a dinner at my house for the whole crew including Sophia and Anthony. I am always hiding little treats like lollipops in my purse for the tiny ones, they are excited to see what Bobby's mom Anna has for them.

Overall, I've had a great experience on this seventeen-year Parenting Partnership journey.

WHAT IS A "NORMAL" FAMILY ANYWAY?

Q: Is there a sense that your family is different from other married couples with children? Does this ever come up with Robert?

Frank and I both come from traditional homes, so we're doing our best to emulate that type of normalcy for Robert. While there have definitely been bumps along the road, I'd say we're doing a great job 90% of the time. We don't always have the same point of view about certain issues, but I'm proud of us and what we've accomplished.

In a Parenting Partnership, the child doesn't know life any other way. Frank and I tried hard to make Robert understand just because two people aren't married or living in the same household doesn't mean they can't have a child. For Robert, the fact that his parents aren't married is completely normal.

He has never obsessed or deeply questioned why Frank and I weren't together—in fact, I don't think he ever saw us as not being together, as we were always in sync in terms of our situation and parenting priorities. Even though Frank and I aren't a couple, we still attend events together—sporting events, school events and plays. We give Robert as much love and support and attention as any other parents give their kids.

Of course, I'm biased because he's my son, but I think Robert is an outstanding young man who is grateful for what he has and appreciates his parents just like his friends who have two married parents, if not more. I feel this is because Frank and I have such a successful, healthy relationship and friendship over these twenty years, especially when compared to some argumentative households. I'd say our kid is calmer, nicer, kinder and more respectful than many children I meet, and I can't imagine him doing any better. Simply put, Parenting Partnership works for us all. Robert knows that I am Mom and Frank is Dad, and this is how our household operates.

A RESOUNDING ENDORSEMENT

Q: Would you recommend that other women consider Parenting Partnerships?

If you're a woman who wants to be a mother but isn't married, I'd 100% recommend looking into a Parenting Partnership. Many women I know who are in traditional marital relationships, for example, can see the advantages. I have a pretty easy life—I get to enjoy having a kid, but there's no angry husband to welcome home from work on a Friday night. I do my own thing and Frank does his own thing, it's a well-orchestrated situation.

I opted not to use a sperm bank because I knew I'd never have a father figure present to help raise my child. Having a father figure makes a real difference in a child's life, especially if you don't have a good support system. Raising a child takes a lot, financially and emotionally. To me, it seems much better to find a partner who wants to be a father and is willing to do that with you.

The other option would be to get married quickly to the next available person you come across. However, don't be surprised if you find yourself clashing with your partner or wanting a divorce soon afterwards. Having a child shouldn't be the focus of a marriage. When getting married, you're looking for a partner for life—and that's not the same.

In addition, I'd advise that you try to avoid becoming a single parent. You'll find yourself arguing with the father of your child for all kinds of reasons. He'll want part of the child; you'll want part of the child. There'll be many child support issues, and no one needs that sort of drama in their life.

Q: What advice would you give to anyone entering a Parenting Partnership?

It's very important to go into a Parenting Partnership with the child as your main priority. Having a baby was always my number one goal in life. It still is, Robert's still my child, after all. For that reason, I don't feel the need to go out and find new boyfriends or a husband. I'm not saying it'll stay this way forever. Now that Robert is getting a bit older, he's definitely becoming more independent, which gives me a chance to change my personal dating scenario. As of this moment, however, I don't have any desire to get into a relationship, much less be in the dating fish bowl. As another single mom recently told me, "It's rough out there."

ROBERT IS MY JOY

Q: How has your son changed your life?

When I was younger, I'd go out, party, and not think about the future—that is, until Bobby came into my life. Being a parent has definitely changed me. I'm a much better person now than I was before, and I keep working to be a better person every day. I want to be as positive and strong as I can now that I'm Robert's mom.

Having children changes people, it made me whole. I truly believe I was born to be a parent. My biggest wish in life was to have a healthy baby. For the most part, that's every parent's main goal. It was an overwhelming success to know that we were able to conceive in the first place, and it felt even better to know all that was ahead of us—Robert has his whole life, while we have our lives as parents and hopefully grandparents. Today, we've created a child with a very strong foundation. In our seventeen-year partnership, Frank and I have never had to deal with ugly custody battles or financial battles, our situation has been overwhelmingly positive.

Q: How do other moms view your Parenting Partnership?

For the most part, being a Parenting Partner hasn't affected my relationship with other moms. Every once in a while, I come into contact with moms who think a woman needs to be married to have children. Obviously, everyone is entitled to their own opinion, but I wouldn't have done things any other way. And I couldn't have.

I wouldn't want to change places with any other mom, even the ones who are married. I know some families who I enjoy being around and, while I value the parents as a strong couple, the wives often seem very critical of their husbands. Some married female friends of mine are even jealous that I have significant personal time and freedom. I only have to do one set of guy's dirty laundry.

Q: What is Robert like?

There's no such thing as a perfect child, but Robert is my perfect. Ever since he was a child, he has always been very curious—we call him Curious George. He enjoys going to school, and he's smart, talkative, and full of questions. Plus, he's super handsome and adorable. He's a jokester, and I love him for it.

Now that he's getting older, he's starting to be more into working to spend and save money. He never used to care about what he looked like, but recently I saw him fixing his hair. Maybe he's got a crush on a girl! Whatever the reason, I love how charismatic he's becoming.

Don't get me wrong, he has his moments, but what kid doesn't? I don't think Robert has a bad bone in his body. He understands the difference between right and wrong. He's respectful, honest, generous with his friends, and has great moments with his brothers. He and his dad have a great relationship. Even though he lives with me most of the time, he spends a lot of time with his dad and sees him as an authority figure. In short, Robert's my entire life. He's everything I've ever wanted and more. I genuinely couldn't imagine my life without him.

Q: What is your relationship with Sophia like?

For the past eleven years, our relationship has improved every year. We get along, but don't go deep with each other. We schedule together on a weekly basis. By far, the highlights have been the mother/son trips together with the boys for a week at a time over spring breaks or during the summer. Sophia plans and executes the entire trip with hotels, cars, airbnbs and cool things to do and see. I truly appreciate her effort as these trips have been a real success every time. Some other fun evenings have occurred when I have hosted dinners where all four boys and all four adults have a large meal together for a special occasion or holiday.

Q: What is your relationship with Natalie like?

I have a lot of respect for Natalie because she embraced supporting Robert in many ways to help him succeed. She and I worked as a team on Robert's middle and high school applications to a number of schools. It was time consuming, we got along great and we executed in a timely manner with Robert getting his top choice school.

Q: Closing comment?

My wish is that every person who is single and knows they want to be a parent can experience the incredible joy of raising a child. If that involves entering into a Parenting Partnership, then I highly recommend it.

CHAPTER 10

SOCIETAL REACTION

Anna and I were entering into a non-traditional relationship to have and raise a child, so we knew we were unlikely to receive the same level of social support afforded to people who enter into traditional marriages the way both of our sets of parents and siblings did when having a child. Most communities, no matter how progressive, tend to look disapprovingly at people who intentionally veer too far from the accepted norm. By entering a Parenting Partnership, we were risking disapproval from our traditionally-minded families and the support of our social networks.

When you are debating entering into a Parenting Partnership you need to discuss with your partner when and to whom you will be revealing your plans. Will you solicit feedback from friends and family before you have even committed to the idea? Will you let them know after you have committed and made some steps towards conception? Will you announce the pregnancy after two, three or four months? When and how you announce is a highly personal decision.

As with many of the choices in life, there are pros and cons to various strategies. Soliciting feedback early on when debating a Parenting Partnership can help you find allies who can help you on your journey and augment your Shared Expectations Document with their sage advice and topics that may not have occurred to you as first time parents. It might help identify potential blindspots about your situation, yourself or your proposed Parenting Partner. However, it can also open you and your partner up to serious negative feedback that could steal your joy and/or sway your thinking with its vitriol.

If you decide to wait to announce, it is likely wise to be sure that the baby is healthy and developing normally. While rarely adhered to in today's age of oversharing on social media, the general rule of thumb on pregnancies is to wait until at least twelve or thirteen weeks before announcing since there is a significantly higher chance of complications during the first trimester. This approach also allows for a stress-free early pregnancy and renders a large portion of potential negative feedback moot.

Whenever you are comfortable sharing this life-altering decision with family and close friends you can express that negative opinions are unwelcome and express your need for a strong support group. There are many decisions to be made when a child is on the way, and it's extremely helpful to be able to talk to those who've already experienced childbirth and raising kids. They can be an outlet for both joy and frustrations and can counsel you when needed.

With Anna's compromised medical situation, we had been advised that she may have a miscarriage during the first four to five months, so it seemed best not to bring anyone else into the situation until we were almost certain that we had a baby coming. As I was thirty-four and she was thirty, we were old enough to make this very private decision on our own. Because Anna was living with her parents they noticed her social and physical changes and started joking that she was pregnant at about three months, but they really got suspicious a few weeks later and pushed her for an answer. She gave in to their guessing when she was three and a half months along. Too much time at home eating and sleeping had given her away. After a little shock and concern, her whole family went into planning mode and a few days later, on Mother's Day 2006 they were spilling over with joy.

Shortly after you announce and again when you have the baby, you'll likely (and hopefully) feel significant positive momentum from almost all of your family and friends with offers of emotional support, time or financial considerations (usually in the form of gifts and hand-me-downs). While they may never be totally accepting of you having a child in a nontraditional manner, a bouncing baby with two committed parents should be a wonderful addition to any family.

In both of my Parenting Partnerships we found the reactions of family, friends and acquaintances ran the gamut from supportive, to indifferent, to skeptical, to directly or indirectly hostile. It is impossible and futile to try to predict family members' reactions in advance, but you should both mentally and emotionally prepare to relish the positives and have perspective about the negative reactions.

MY PARENTS REACTIONS

It was understandably upsetting to my parents that they were unaware of my agreement with Anna and the pregnancy until I told them when we were five months along. In hindsight, Anna and I likely could have brought in select people earlier, but we didn't want to get our families excited in case anything went wrong. A grandparent's excitement is very different from that of a younger family member or a friend, it's much more personal, since they think of the new baby in terms of their direct lineage and life fulfillment. I also had held off telling my family because I assumed (correctly this time) that some of them would have difficulty with the decision Anna and I had made. My parents, while not ultra-conservative, were certainly not progressive enough to immediately get behind the concept of a Parenting Partnership. This made it extra important for me to share the news in person, which circumstances prevented until fairly late in the pregnancy.

When I did tell my parents the news, I tried to be very thorough and straightforward about it. I took them through the steps of what had happened and why. I explained Anna's issues, that she'd asked me to have a child with her over a year ago, that we took six months to decide and that we had a baby on the way with a due date in four months. I pressed to get the whole story across —detailing Anna's medical difficulties, exploring other options, not willing to force a marriage, our nontraditional solution, planned conception, risky pregnancy, excitement for the baby, and commitment to be parents for life. As I'd anticipated, my parents' initial reactions were negative, they thought it was weird and kept their emotional distance. They interrupted, judged and debated throughout the "conversation."

My parents got married when they were both twenty-one years old in 1969, having two children by twenty-five years of age. Prior to their marriage they each dated a handful of people, in most instances without premarital sex, a typical scenario for their generation and the moral- and marriage-focused culture of those times. Because of their experience, they didn't have a lot in common with the experience of a highly independent thirty-year-old woman with a medical deadline and a thirty-four-year-old, well-traveled, unmarried man who both wanted a child, but didn't require marriage.

My mom, who is conservative and religious, took issue with us not being married. At the same time, she was also upset that she hadn't been involved in the pregnancy process at all. She said she would have wanted to throw baby showers and other celebratory events (not that it could not happen at this point, but there were distance issues and such). I could tell she was also concerned about the future ramifications of the Parenting Partnership. Our arrangement—intentionally having a child outside of wedlock—seemed to tap into all the negative associations she had with divorce. She'd been subjected to split family dynamics through my dad's family and it was always uncomfortable for her on multiple levels: bickering, the example set for her kids, logistical hassles, and having extra holiday locations. As someone who's family prided itself on never having any divorces and having worked very hard to save her own marriage, she did not approve. My father was much more pragmatic about the situation than my mom—overall he was happy about the prospect of more grandchildren—but he felt hurt that he hadn't been involved in the decision-making process from the beginning. While he didn't have as rigid a definition of family as my mom, seeing as he had experienced multiple divorces, step-siblings and half-siblings on his side of the family, the concept of a Parenting Partnership was still foreign to him at first.

With much time passing, and now that I'm a dad of four, I can understand their concerned and hurt reactions—as a parent, you'd like to think that your child would come to you for wisdom about a life-altering decision regardless of their age. As a parent you want your children to share the same deeply-held values that you believe to be sacrosanct and have fought for in your life. At the time their reactions were less than I would have liked. I was hoping for joy and big picture validation. Looking back, I should have understood that they needed time to process the surprise announcement and not have hoped they would mirror my excitement. It takes time for people to open their mind to ideas that are foreign to them. Additionally, I had been getting comfortable with the Parenting Partnership concept for over a year and they just heard about it ten minutes ago. Along with not understanding and not agreeing, their reaction also suffered from some embarrassment. When I consider the situation from their perspective, I can completely sympathize—imagine having to tell your family and friends that you've just found out that your eldest son is going to have a grandchild in four months. Announcements like these can lead to many false assumptions, especially from friends who come from that older generation and background. In the end, I don't fault them for reacting the way they did, but certainly wish Parenting Partnerships were a mainstream concept that could have been more quickly relatable.

One other strong positive was that they had known Anna for a number of years and were familiar with her strong maternal qualities.

SIBLING REACTION

My two much younger millennial-era brothers, who were unmarried twenty- and eighteen-year-olds at the time, couldn't have cared less about the unconventionality of my situation and loved the idea of more young kids in the family. That could not be said for my two-years younger sister. While similar in age to myself at thirty-two and squarely a Gen X'er like me, her reaction was likely the most negative of all.

Similar to my parents, she married young at twenty-four, had already had a son and two daughters by the time we announced and had always lived her life in a conventional, "by the rules" manner. Her reaction to the news of my Parenting Partnership seemed to hinge a lot on how her two young daughters would process the situation. As hard as it was for her to comprehend my situation, she didn't know how to explain the situation to them and seemed worried about the example she perceived we were setting. As you can imagine, this reaction only intensified when she had another daughter soon after and I had another son via Parenting Partnership five years later.

Obviously, people have different experiences and viewpoints which can cause tension within a family. I recognized how difficult it was for the three of them to understand and the pressure they felt to explain it to others. There were also lots of unknowns for them, since Anna and I had forged this new path together. They were at the same starting point with learning and understanding this new dynamic as I had been almost eighteen months earlier. It helped me to remember that people bring their own lens to every situation. None of them had ever been in Anna's scenario or lived my life, so they didn't properly understand what led to our decisions. Even though they are all bright people, very few can quickly process something that is so distant from their own life choices in a short time. Sadly, in over seventeen years since I told them, only my father has really been able to swing most of the way around on the topic of Parenting Partnerships. My mother, while loving towards the older boys and cordial to the Parenting Partners, still makes her overall disapproval of the situation known to me frequently. The fracture with my sister has still not yet healed.

NOT EVERYONE WILL UNDERSTAND

It can be hard to tell others about Parenting Partnerships, as it's a situation that most people won't understand or ever need to consider in their own life. Some passionately dislike the idea, others don't believe in it, and others simply don't really care about understanding your life at all. There are still others that are completely supportive. I have found that divorced single mothers are the most positive and open to the concepts of Parenting Partnerships. Likewise, divorced men, both with and without kids are also quite positive, but usually for more dubious reasons.

In all honesty, most people don't understand Parenting Partnerships for three reasons:

1. It is a unique situation with which they have no context or familiarity.

2. It is a somewhat complex, highly personal situation that they've never contemplated.

3. It is contrary to the mainstream ideal pushing marriage first for all child conception.

When it does come up socially, most people will ask a polite question, but if you choose to follow up with a detailed and somewhat lengthy description, they really didn't want that much info. In fact, many don't want to hear an explanation at all—I'm always surprised when people ask a question about an obviously personal subject, but won't give the few minutes time to hear the story and instead stick to their preconceived judgments. Parenting Partnerships are not THAT overly complicated. It has gotten to the point where I either answer with one sentence, "We partner as parents with no romantic involvement," or if they seem to have genuine interest I ask them for ten to fifteen minutes of their time to explain it properly in a quiet environment and field their inevitable follow up questions.

Personally, I think our story is extremely endearing. A woman with a pressing medical issue asks someone from her past to have a child with her because she has a lifelong, deep desire for her own child. Together they come up with a unique way to accomplish this shared lifetime goal. If I was a third party who'd never been in a Parenting Partnership or heard of Anna or Sophia's situation, I believe I'd be empathetic, curious and complimentary. Of those who are interested, only a very small segment of people will fully understand your decision. There have been very few people who really cared or had the capacity to fathom and be positive.

DON'T JUDGE

To the people who say Parenting Partnerships are wrong, bizarre, weird, or untenable my response is very clear—they're misinformed. Parenting Partnerships are just another way two people have chosen to live their life. You can advocate that a person should follow a traditional path and get married, but you can't dictate it. You can't insist that marriage equates to having children. Just because a person may have ruled out the idea of marriage, that doesn't mean they don't desire to have children or lack the makeup to effectively parent.

It has been my observation that the people who most vehemently dismiss Parenting Partnerships are the unhappily married; stuck in negative, confining marriages that they "settled" into "because it was time to get married" or "time to have children." Embittered across the board, but clinging to "doing the right thing." It's human nature to distance ourselves from concepts significantly different from the choices we have made, especially if you secretly rue those decisions. I recognize they feel pride and accomplishment in some aspects of their marriage, but that doesn't mean they should criticize the decisions and life choices of others. Whatever their reasons, just remember that their opinions have no bearing on you or how you raise your child.

When talking to outsiders about your Parenting Partnership, it's important not to invest too much emotional capital in trying to make them understand. If someone's trapped in a certain mindset and thinks Parenting Partnerships are wrong, nothing will change their mind in the short term. Even those who don't judge you can be quick to say they'd never follow the same path. This might be easy for them to say, but the truth is they have no idea what they would have done if they'd had the same experiences: a biological clock that's running out, not finding a true match marital partner, not fitting the hetero-normative perspective, having a strong aversion to marriage, or experiencing medical issues. You never know what you'd decide or how you'd behave until you're put in a certain situation.

SOCIAL PRESSURE

Social reactions can prove to be more of a concern in situations where your child's well-being is impacted because someone doesn't like that "the child's parents aren't married." There are certainly married couples that will not socialize with, or allow their children to socialize with, single parents.

In general, though, the fact that people judge us doesn't bother me. I've been through it a million times before as an entrepreneur. Anna, on the other hand, had a tough time at first adjusting to the partnership. Now, however, she's an expert on all of the advantages. When asked about her situation, Anna can easily explain the advantages of a Parenting Partnership compared to other arrangements.

In fact, our relationship has lasted longer than many of the married couples we know. Seventeen years into our Parenting Partnership, we still get on well, attend high school events together and interact socially with friends and family. As partners, we're in a much better place than some of the people who judged us. It turns out that we were criticized by people who weren't happy with themselves and isn't that almost always the case?

When people meet Robert, there's no way they can doubt the effectiveness of Anna's and my situation. Anyone who's met him will tell you what a sweet, kind and well-adjusted young man he has become. Before he was born, however, these same people might have predicted that he'd be maladjusted and "messed up." In fact, he is the kind of kid that other parents want their kids to hang out with. As I'll cover in the next chapter, all of these same attributes, both positive and negative apply to how Sophia and Anthony are viewed.

Like most parents I am biased, but I have to say that both my boys are absolutely fantastic and well integrated in every sense. This is a point of pride and validation for our Parenting Partnerships.

CHAPTER 11

MY SECOND PARENTING PARTNERSHIP

In the summer of 2004 I moved to Texas. After a few months of getting settled in, I met and started casually dating a woman named Sophia in November 2004. Timeline-wise, this was a month after I was told about Anna's ectopic pregnancy which occurred in October of 2004 and while Anna was finding out more about her reproductive health issues both related and unrelated to the ectopic pregnancy.

Sophia was working post-college in the medical field while preparing to enter nursing school. With Anna's permission and as appropriate, I related some aspects of Anna's medical ordeal, which Sophia received with genuine interest as it was an ongoing, significant medical situation. When Anna first asked me to consider having a child with her in 2005,

I immediately mentioned her request and my subsequent reluctance to Sophia seeing as we were dating.

Sophia's overall reaction to the initial request was and was not what one would expect. Sophia, a millennial, felt a deep level of compassion for Anna even though the two had never met. She thought the overall idea had merit and even encouraged me to explore it further. Sophia knew I had a strong desire to have children and that was not something that was on her radar in the near future due to her dream of nursing school and a career in healthcare. Once I decided to move forward with a Parenting Partnership with Anna in 2005, Sophia and I stopped dating.

As I've said before, being in a Parenting Partnership significantly reshapes your romantic parameters. In my experience, it effectively eliminates the possibility of a semi-serious relationship. Either you say you're dating casually without the intention of getting married or having a child (as Sophia and I were at the time), or you find someone who loves you so much that they can accept you, your child and your Parenting Partnership (as was the case years later with my wife Natalie)—there's really no middle ground.

WAKING UP IN THE EMERGENCY ROOM

In summer of 2008, Sophia woke up one morning with a pain in her lower abdomen, followed by uncontrollable internal bleeding.[86] She called 911. She passed out from the pain. The next thing she remembers is waking up in the emergency room.

The EMTs had found her in a pool of her own blood. The doctors informed her that one of her ovaries had ruptured which caused the bleeding and her near death. She received a couple pints of blood and was in recovery for a day, then had to undergo surgery to remove the ruined half of an ovary that remained. They told her that the cause was cystic growths. While she had survived that terrible event, there was more awful news to follow. The cysts that had destroyed one of her ovaries and almost killed her were present on her other ovary as well. This meant that the remaining ovary could rupture at any moment. Should that happen, not only would she be in another life-threatening situation, but she would never be able to have children of her own. Another surgery followed shortly to remove some of the cysts from the remaining ovary. The medical term for what afflicted Sophia was Polycystic Ovary Syndrome (PCOS). The CDC estimates that PCOS affects 6-12% of US women of reproductive age. While it is treatable once detected, it nonetheless is one of the most common causes of female infertility.[87]

Polycystic ovary

Uterus

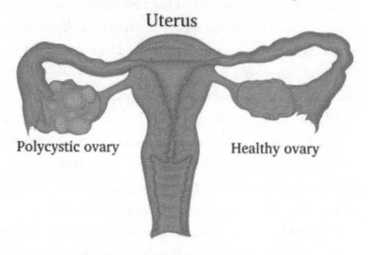

Polycystic ovary   Healthy ovary

For a twenty-five-year-old woman, this was a major blow. While she didn't necessarily have the same narrow window of opportunity that Anna had been given after her medical ordeal, her situation was just as precarious, if not more so. She was definitely confronting an unexpected limitation on her ability to have a biological child. Given what she knew about me, and our fairly recent history together, she thought of asking if I'd consider doing the same thing with her that I'd done with Anna.

I don't believe in jumping into Parenting Partnerships without plenty of thought, discussion, and soul searching. I also believe that for most people, one Parenting Partnership should meet their needs and be more than enough. The fact that I was already in a Parenting Partnership might have been a reason to say no to Sophia's request. For me, it was actually a reason to say yes. I'd had a positive experience in all ways with Anna, and I was over the moon with Robert. The profound changes that fatherhood brought were welcomed as I truly enjoyed all aspects of being a father. Robert, then four-years-old, was an absolute joy and the thought of giving him a sibling was yet another strong positive.

Bottom line, I'd done this once before and seen that it worked well so I was considerably more open-minded to the idea of doing it again. Because Sophia had been in my life previously, she was already familiar with many of the details of Parenting Partnerships. Still, we didn't rush into it. Sophia and I decided we would start the discussions once she had a little distance from her medical trauma and I had time to process for myself and discuss with Anna.

SETTING EXPECTATIONS WITH SOPHIA

I went through a similar list of considerations with Sophia that I'd gone through with Anna. I'd learned a lot from my pre-partnership conversations with Anna, which made talking to Sophia much more straightforward. While some of our conversations went the same way (for example, Sophia had no issue with our child having my last name), there were some significant differences that had to be addressed for the first time.

Sophia and Anna are two very different people with two different backgrounds. For instance, since Sophia is a Texas native she has a lot of family living nearby and a large group of friends from high school and college, all of whom are very involved in her life and many of whom have children of similar ages. This gave her a large community of support that would positively impact her experience as a parent. At the same time, it meant finding time to integrate our child into my family would be more difficult than what I experienced with Anna and Robert since Sophia had an equally strong desire to do the same with her own family and friends. Another difference was Sophia's disdain for living in the city and preference for the suburbs. The compromise on this was picking a suburb that was on the same side of town as my office/home and Anna and Robert's home.

Another new topic during expectation setting was my need to solidify Sophia's commitment to making every effort to bond the two would-be siblings; the new baby and Robert. I loved having siblings growing up and I was thrilled that this second Parenting Partnership would allow my two children to have that same joy. If I was going to have a child with Sophia, I needed a documented, firm, unwavering commitment from Sophia that she would actively help the two children spend a lot of time together in concert with Anna and me.

Ultimately, the discussion phase gave Sophia and me the opportunity to evaluate the same things Anna and I had had to evaluate. Key Point #1 - whether we are ready as individuals. Key Point #2 - whether we had faith in the other person's ability to be a great parent. For Sophia, she'd seen evidence that I was a kind parent and a committed Parenting Partner. I likewise was sure of Sophia's ardent commitment.

Key Point #3 - the documentation of legal items and Shared Expectations.

TRAGEDY AND JOY

Sophia and my journey has had its share of difficulties. Unlike my experience with Anna, our initial attempts to conceive resulted in a miscarriage. It was a tragic and heartbreaking loss for both of us. We took it very hard, but did our best to overcome this devastating loss because we knew we wanted to be parents together. Professional counseling and support from family and friends can be helpful in overcoming a lost pregnancy. It's important to remind yourself that conception doesn't always work. It is estimated that as many as 26% of all pregnancies end in miscarriage and up to 10% of clinically recognized pregnancies[88] (visualized on an ultrasound, fetal heartbeat, confirmed by high levels of hCG or pregnancy tissue detected after a loss).[89] Miscarriages happen, and they're emotionally devastating. Would you be willing to try to conceive again with your partner if you suffered a miscarriage set back? What if you needed a medically-induced miscarriage? How many attempts would you make? These questions and more should be part of your initial conception conversations.

Thankfully, a successful pregnancy resulted in Sophia giving birth to Anthony, her first child and my second son. We were fortunate to have a healthy child, which alleviated 98% of our overwhelming concerns. Most everything went very well for Sophia, Anthony and me over the first few years.

OTHER TOUGH TIMES OVER THE FIRST 11 YEARS

My two Parenting Partnerships have gone extremely well and are getting even better with each passing year. But, nothing is perfect and many people want to hear about the tough times. So here is a list of the hurdles we have overcome.

The first hurdle actually happened before Robert was born in early 2006. As with any pregnancy, Anna's OBGYN performed a routine STD check. The results showed a positive for a common STD. She called me concerned and angry. I immediately went to get tested and was not positive for that STD. This caused a significant short-term crisis for both of us. Ultimately, Anna was quickly retested and the result was negative, confirming the original test was a false-positive. That was a very difficult week and highlighted the seriousness of having trust, strong communication, and responsible partners.

The second and third hurdles were during Anthony's first year. Sophia was very much in a nesting phase and surrounded by her many local family members so she felt less urgency to immediately incorporate Anna and five-year-old Robert than I or they would have liked. Reflecting back, even though "integrating the brothers" was of the highest priority in our Shared Expectation Document, my expectations should have been lower regarding the brother's interactions in the baby's first twelve to eighteen months. Meeting the mother's nesting needs and honoring her preferences postpartum is essential for any parenting couple. There is no way to predict what this will entail.

The third hurdle was Anna's growing concern that there would be a resource management issue due to Sophia and Anthony. Anna felt threatened which is understandable when someone new shows up with a claim on the other partner's time and resources.

Ultimately both of these early issues melted away. Anna did not experience any significant change in my time or resources devoted to Robert. And once Anthony was a little older Sophia was more open to visits and outings, which was accelerated by an extended stay from my mother. Ever since that family-motivated icebreaker the moms began arranging to have the boys meet up with one another sporadically and then weekly. Nowadays, we are years removed from any awkwardness during the initial integration and have had no significant friction between the two moms.

Furthermore, video calls happen regularly between all parties. Sleepovers too. As Anna mentioned, she and Sophia have even taken spring break and summer vacations together—just the two moms and the two boys! While they are not "best friends," they get along well, support each other quite a bit, frequently take the boys to hang out at each other's houses and treat each other with deep respect. Since providing an environment for healthy, happy children is everyone's number one goal, they are outwardly supportive and positive with both boys for the sake of their brotherhood.

A fourth hurdle for me is balancing attention, praise and time between the two children. When Anthony was born there was certainly an adjustment period for Robert, who was five years older. Like any former "only child" he was used to getting all the attention all the time and he wasn't fond of sharing the spotlight nor his dad with this new sibling. I do my best to make sure I see both of my boys equally, sometimes together and other times just one-on-one. It's a challenge that I'm happy to attack and you'll read about some of the strategies I use in the upcoming chapters. Spending time with them individually and seeing them spend time together are some of the top moments in my life. This is still a lingering issue to this day that requires attention.

A fifth hurdle years later was when Sophia seriously dated, got engaged and moved Anthony into a new home. Sophia wanted to create a clear separation between her new relationship status and the two Parenting Partnerships. This was well within her rights and covered in our Shared Expectations Document so we didn't have a fundamental conflict, but we did have some communication and scheduling misunderstandings because Sophia was no longer free-flowing and over-communicating details of her and Anthony's schedule and whereabouts. Additionally, some financial support needed to be adjusted to reflect this new reality and those conversations were a bit tense. Unfortunately that relationship did not work out and Sophia and Anthony moved back into a home of their own.

A sixth hurdle was our toughest self-inflicted wound. Sophia ran up a balance on a personal credit card and started withdrawing cash monthly from the childcare account to pay the minimum balance. While we have experienced more tragic events in our partnerships—the medical troubles and miscarriage tragedies—the deceit and lying around this financial impropriety caused the most negativity. The fallout from this was wide-reaching as it ultimately affected where Sophia and Anthony lived, where Anthony was schooled for one year, accelerated Sophia's timeline to return to full-time work and all future financial interactions between the two of us.

The incidents above and Sophia's miscarriage are the toughest times we've had through two Parenting Partnerships over seventeen years. For the past four years we have not had any significant issues and have all grown much closer with no storm clouds on the horizon. While unfortunate, all of these negatives don't compare at all to the joy and love that has been added to our lives through Robert and Anthony. Also, overcoming these setbacks has strengthened our Parenting Partnership ecosystem.

ECOSYSTEM

For Anna and Sophia they provide singularly focused love and attention on their sons and show every indication that they are completely enamored with their children. In a very positive twist, a strong bond has even developed between Robert and Anthony's mother Sophia and between Anthony and Robert's mom Anna. Furthermore, both of my Parenting Partners adore the boys' two little brothers Nicolas and Nathan, and have been so kind with hand-me-downs, treats, gifts, and positivity. Natalie and I list Anna and Sophia as emergency contacts for our sitters, for schools, and on medical forms. Both of my sons' moms are an extension of our core family ecosystem. Robert and Anthony are members of the family, and by extension Anna and Sophia are often invited to family activities, holiday gatherings and special occasions. The inclusive nature of our ecosystem might be an outlier for Parenting Partnerships. I'm not sure you can expect it to be the norm in all situations, however, at the bare minimum, Parenting Partners should treat each other with utmost respect both for their important position in the family ecosystem and as an example to set for your child. You are all a team, working together for the best interest of your children.

CHAPTER 12

FINDING LOVE POST-PARENTING PARTNERSHIPS

In 2012 I was forty years old. Feeling very settled with a successful career and two amazing sons. I had purpose. I had a legacy. I was getting and giving unconditional love. I had personal freedom. I really didn't need more from life. There was no pull to find a serious relationship—much less a marriage—to be happy. I was already very fulfilled, moving past any preprogrammed need for a marriage as a way to justify, or prop up, my life. I, for certain, wasn't going to get caught up in a sub par relationship. Unless something extraordinary came along, I was happy on my own.

Then, I met Natalie.

After our fairly funny first meeting and first date experiences, I immediately knew we were right for one another. Never had I dropped down to one knee and presented a ring to anyone, but that all changed after a few years of serious dating when I asked Natalie to marry me. We've been dating and married for over ten years and are as strong as ever. Natalie and I were married in 2017 and had our boys Nicolas and Nathan in 2019 and 2020.

Having two children from two different Parenting Partnerships didn't make it impossible for me to find love, quite the contrary. When I was not watching the boys I had true personal time plus a clarity of purpose and a high level of intensity. This created a healthy, very high bar for serious romantic involvements.

Once you have a child (from a Parenting Partnership or otherwise) life, work and dating definitely morph from light-hearted to serious adulting. This is the main reason why I wouldn't recommend entering into a Parenting Partnership until you're in your thirties or forties, unless you have an extreme medical situation like Anna and Sophia.

Being in a Parenting Partnership allows each partner the flexibility to have their own social life, and perhaps to start dating someone who becomes a long-term romantic partner that eventually grows into a marriage. It leaves the door open, so to speak. By having a Parenting Partnership, you still have the opportunity, and in many ways a better chance, to meet the precise right person for you.

MEETING NATALIE

For me personally, that's how it worked. Had I made different life choices earlier in my life, such as getting into a suboptimal marriage to have kids, I would probably not have had the opportunity to meet and marry the love of my life. My Parenting Partners still have the chance, and I hope they, too, will find the love of their lives and get married. Optionality is a highly valuable element of any Parenting Partnership. You have the right to date, but don't feel the pressure to commit for negative reasons or force a marriage. So you can spend time searching for romantic happiness from the safe nest of parenting, love, and responsibility.

I admit that having two Parenting Partnerships, and two children with two different women, did take some getting used to for Natalie. At times it has put added stress on our relationship. We had many back and forth discussions about my situation, just like any other couple would when there are kids involved. While Natalie had previously been married and divorced, a Parenting Partnership was a foreign concept to her, and it was some work on her side to accept the additional complexity. After all, no little girl has ever said to herself that she wants to grow up to marry a partner who has two children with two different people. It certainly did not fit the mainstream or fairytale model of relationships or her more traditional Texas views.

Ultimately, our communication and love won out as Natalie was able to find understanding and give acceptance. I don't like the term baggage, but it's become a popular term in our society for a reason—if single people don't have any baggage, it's quite the commitment for them to get involved with someone who has a child and/or ex-spouse. However, by the time you're in your thirties or forties, as I was when I met Natalie, many people who are dating have already been married, divorced, or had kids, so it's far less likely to be a deal breaking issue.

However, you still need to ask yourself, will this person love my children? Will they share in parenting my child? How do I expect my future spouse to interact with my Parenting Partner? Do they accept and/or respect the agreements I've made with my Parenting Partner? And many other questions...

ANNA AND SOPHIA

My Parenting Partners have differing views on dating. For Anna, dating is very low on her priority list. She really enjoys being social, but she's fulfilled caring for Robert and hanging out with other parents from his school and their neighborhood. Sophia, as mentioned, got seriously involved and engaged at one point. She wasn't overly forthright about the relationship at first, partly because she wasn't sure where it was going, and partly because she wasn't sure how I'd react. For example, she worried I could have reacted negatively which she believed would impact my financial contributions above and beyond my legal requirements.

Her fears were unfounded as I was happy for Sophia—I'd long been mentally prepared for Anna or her to date other people and hopefully get married. Naturally, I did and would have a parent's normal concerns. First of all, I wanted to be sure that this man had the best intentions and certainly wasn't an abuser, a pedophile, or poor role model. It might sound jaded or harsh to some, but a parent should always be vigilant to the extreme about the safety of their child. I also wanted to be sure that, if he and Sophia did decide to commit, he was prepared to love Anthony, and that they would always factor in Robert's and my relationship with Anthony.

As it happened, Sophia's relationship came to an end. She states that she is still open to dating and we all fully expect her to find her awesome partner soon enough. Everyone—friends, family, sons, me, Natalie—genuinely hope that both Sophia and Anna are able to find long-term romantic partners.

CHAPTER 13

NATALIE'S EXPERIENCE

Beyond my two positive Parenting Partnerships with Anna and Sophia I was able to find an amazing marital relationship with Natalie. We have all worked hard to establish respectful relationships so we can raise incredible children. It *is* possible. This chapter is an interview with Natalie:

Q: When you began dating Frank, how long was it before he told you about his Parenting Partnership arrangements? What was your reaction?

> Frank told me about Anna and Sophia at dinner on our second date. My reaction was a pie chart of interest, nonjudgmental thoughts, judgmental thoughts and curiosity. I certainly wanted to hear more.

Q: Had you ever heard of such an arrangement before?

Nope! Hence the reactions above! Although my family was not "traditional" in most senses, most of our complexities were common. My parents divorced when I was four. They both remarried and I became a stepdaughter and stepsister. My extended family also experienced divorces, deaths, remarriage and adoptions, so a re-structured or blended family was familiar to me.

Q: Frank has shared that you have become quite close with his Parenting Partners. Tell us more about that.

"Closeness" is a subjective term. It's inevitable to become "close" to some degree when you are partnering to care for a child. When needed, I have a close working relationship with Anna and Sophia in regards to the children. I am not personally close with either, although one relationship is more positive than the other. Over time, my level of comfort and relationship with both has improved. The complexities of personalities, preferences, and agreements will determine a significant other's level of closeness as the significant other of people participating in a Parenting Partnership. It is in the best interest of the boys for us to exhibit a cohesive, harmonious dynamic—me especially. So whenever I'm participating or coordinating with the Parenting Partners, that is what I have in mind. Creating a scenario that is comfortable, fun, and relaxed for the kids, that gives them space to feel loved and supported by this ecosystem that cares for them. For example, the kids wanted to go to Disney World and wanted both parents to share that joy. Frank and I believed that it would be an important memory for the children and made the decision to take everyone, since sharing that special time was best for the kids.

Q: If a spouse chose not to be close with a Parenting Partner, how might that affect the family dynamics and the marriage?

It depends on what the agreement between the spouses is—what they decide their dynamics with a Parenting Partner will be and what best serves their family unit. A spouse can choose not to be close with a Parenting Partner and still maintain a courteous, respectful, and overall positive relationship that benefits the children. Also keep in mind that a Parenting Partner may not be open to closeness. In any scenario, both parties should focus on healthy and respectful communication to facilitate a nurturing environment for the children. As long as the spouses are aligned on their expectations for this relationship, the family and marital dynamics should not be negatively affected.

Q: What is the most complicated part of being married to someone who has a Parenting Partnership?

At this point in our relationship, scheduling. Coordinating four adults, one highschooler, one middle schooler, and two toddlers can be difficult. Early in our relationship, the difficulties manifested more emotionally and financially. Change is difficult, and navigating the changes and phases of life takes introspection, patience, and realistic goal setting. As we all know, you cannot control another person—attitude or actions or anything, really. When I was "just a girlfriend", the Parenting Partners were dismissive of and negative toward my relationship with Frank. As our relationship continued and our commitment outwardly proven, the interactions mildly improved. However, a true shift in attitudes and acceptance did not happen until about five years into our relationship when we were married. Even then, since Frank and I did not have children, our relationship was still marginalized. At this point, eleven years in and with two children, my relationship with the Parenting Partners is at its healthiest. I believe that we all truly have the best interest of the kids in mind, and have grown and matured to overcome any of our own insecurities or hesitancies and will continue to improve as parents and partners.

Q: What is your role in parenting Frank's other children?

I am a facilitator. I am a secondary figure in the time spent with their dad, meaning I do things that support positive and fun interactions and experiences for Frank and the older boys. Additionally, I also facilitate experiences for the two older boys to have with their little brothers. For example, if Dad is finishing a meeting, I'll take the boys to ride bikes or breakfast so they are free to play when we get back. I'll also schedule an event for all six of us so all the children can have new experiences together. Sometimes it's simply about taking care of basic needs like making sure we have their favorite snacks. I also help navigate discipline, but ultimately have Frank shape those conversations and actions and support his decisions. That said, I am also aware that as children grow and change, what they need from me will change as well. In our scenario, both boys were young when Frank and I began our relationship. My interactions have evolved from helping them to the potty, orchestrating backyard bonanzas, to writing essays for high school applications. I have had conversations over the years about what I can do to be a bonus in their lives. I take those to heart and try to implement those suggestions when possible.

Q: Do you have any advice or words of wisdom for people who might choose to marry a spouse who has a Parenting Partner?

Of highest importance—read this book!! After that, frequent, open, in-depth conversations with your spouse. Facilitate group meetings with all parents involved to ensure everyone understands the Parenting Partnership situation and responsibilities. There are so many questions to ask along the way, and answers that may need clarifying as your relationship evolves. Ask the hard questions early. Understand that you are shaping young lives and that you should lead by example.

CHAPTER 14

FUNDAMENTAL AND IMPORTANT INTERACTIONS WITHIN THE ECOSYSTEM

As you can tell, we are near the end of the book and you may still be thinking, "This seems straightforward, very doable, and fairly drama-free. Did I miss something?" You did not miss anything and we want to reinforce your overall positive feelings to confirm your correct conclusion. Two mature adults entering into a Parenting Partnership and having one child can be everything you've dreamed of. Even my over-the-top situation has brought the highest-of-highs without the lowest-of-lows.

What does a normal week look like for all parties involved? How do the boys get along with one another? How do the four parents make it work? How do you explain it all to your child? This chapter covers our common interactions to maintain a positive ecosystem around the boys.

SCHOOL ROUTINE

Let's start with Sunday evening at 7:30pm. No matter where they have been or what they have been up to, the boys are back at their mothers' homes for a good night's sleep before school on Monday. Obviously, each Parenting Partnership is going to be different, but generally speaking the child is going to spend the majority of the weekdays at either one parent or the other's to establish an efficient school routine. With the demands of high school and junior high, both boys presently sleep at their mothers' Sunday through Thursday. When they were younger they would occasionally sleep over at dad's during the week. Anthony still does sometimes when Sophia has a work trip. Robert, a sophomore, now carpools to and from school. On Wednesdays and Fridays I pick up Anthony at 3pm. Robert will usually come over on those days after his extracurriculars at about 5:30. We spend the evenings doing homework, hanging out, playing with the little brothers, and having dinner. This normalcy provides stability. An important part of a successful Parenting Partnership is creating a healthy routine and dependable environment for the kids. Sophia will stop by to pick up Anthony on Wednesday after work at about 8pm. On Fridays, and sometimes Saturdays, both boys stay the night and return to their mothers the subsequent day for dinner or activities with their school friends.

Weekends are valuable time, right? Everyone is off work and has a couple of days to do whatever they want. Our legal document specifies that we rotate weekends, but our Shared Expectations Document expressed a desire for more frequent, albeit shorter, interactions. This is a preference between the partners that is important to specify. We generally enact a split weekend model with each parent having one night and day so neither parent goes too long without quality time with their child. Splitting weekend nights benefits the parents as well; allowing Parenting Partners to have their own separate lives and pursue social events, friendships, and hobbies. If I know I have the boys on Friday, I'll schedule a date night with my wife or plans with my friends on Saturday night. Other parents enact a "one week on / one week off" custody while yet others have their child staying full time at only one home.

In addition to this overall routine, we also have incorporated a great deal of flexibility which includes a "heads-up-I'll-be-stopping-by" policy. This allows either parent to ask to drop-in for a quick connection—ice cream run, hug and kiss, thirty minute hangout—when time allows and we are nearby. Logistics and geography play a large role in this routine and flexibility. Robert lives just three minutes away, so he doesn't spend the night as much. He comes over, we spend time together, and he often goes back home because it's nearby and he's particular about his sleeping arrangements (little brothers wake him easily). Anthony, on the other hand, lives nineteen minutes away. So, it's just more convenient for him to spend the night more often. Plus, Sophia is independent and she likes free time to herself so she's content letting Anthony spend the night more regularly. Anna prefers to have Robert come back to spend the night at her house. As I said before, every Parenting Partnership is different, and you'll figure out which type of routine works best for your child and the parents.

Generally, I overlap my time with the boys so that they get time with one another as well. They are brothers and I want them to grow up close. This won't apply to most Parenting Partnerships, but will if either Parenting Partner had a child previously. When I plan something fun like a special excursion to the zoo or the science center I always try to take both boys. Should the boys not be able to overlap, that is fine as well since one-on-one time with each child needs to occur.

As Anthony got older, he and Robert became much closer because they could now interact and play with each other in a typical manner: sports, events, card games, horseplay, video games, movies, ganging up on dad, and annoying one another. These days, they do all the brotherly stuff and are completely bonded. We have family dinners together, take day trips, watch Robert's baseball games, and have water balloon fights. Robert and Anthony's relationship is my proudest accomplishment. At my house, they have shared bunk beds for years. Through weekly scheduling, about 80% of the visits to dad's place include both Robert and Anthony at the same time. This maximizes their time together and continues to grow and reinforce their bond.

BIRTHDAYS, HOLIDAYS, SUMMER AND VACATIONS

You might think that birthdays, holidays and vacations would be a cause for friction between Parenting Partners. Nope. Recall that this is set forth in writing in the custody documents and Shared Expectations Document. Plus, everyone gets along well enough that all the parents are usually invited to holiday dinners, local family gatherings, and so on. For birthdays we'll usually arrange two birthday celebrations with one on the actual day and the other the weekend before or after. Living close by allows the boys to attend two Thanksgiving dinners or Christmases in one day if needed.

For example, during the 2021 winter holiday both Robert and Anthony came over for the full day on December 24th and opened a couple gifts with their two little brothers, returning to their mothers' homes that evening so they could have Christmas morning with their moms. They opened a present or two and interacted with their mothers' families either in person or by video chat. Late afternoon, Natalie, myself, and the two youngest boys packed a couple more gifts and a cake and headed to Anna and Robert's for a Christmas dinner. Sophia and Anthony met us there and all six of us watched as the two youngest brothers ripped through packages and thoroughly enjoyed themselves. On December 26th, the four brothers, Natalie and I boarded a flight to see my extended family, returning Robert and Anthony to their moms for New Years Eve festivities.

As stated, it is a key part of our Shared Expectations Document that the boys would be well integrated with my extended family. When my family is in town I want the boys to spend extra time and bond with them. The Parenting Partners have been great about being flexible when grandparents or other family have visited, as have I with their extended families.

Vacations are very important bonding opportunities. Some have been with both boys and others just one-on-one. We had a ton of fun fishing in Louisiana and traveling to Atlanta and Florida to see our favorite teams play. We always make sure to visit the local universities to see the campus and buy some swag. Our family road trip went from Texas to Indiana stopping to see family in Dallas, Graceland and Bass Pro Shop flagship in Memphis, the Grand Ole Opry in Nashville, and our cousin's on a lake in Indiana.

As Natalie mentioned, and before the little brothers were born, we had a joint vacation with everyone to Disney World, which was awesome. Anna and Sophia flew there early with their boys. Those four spent two days exploring Orlando without me and Natalie around. Then, Natalie and I arrived and all six of us experienced Disney together. The moms then left, giving Natalie and I the second half of the vacation to bond with the boys and take them to visit their grandparents and cousins. Robert and Anthony spent quality time with their parents, had brother bonding time, met Mickey and saw their extended family!

COMMUNICATION IS KEY

As you have heard a thousand times, communication is key! Totally true. The smooth routine and slick vacation planning mentioned above require significant ecosystem communication. There are lengthy sit downs and endless micro-interactions necessary to make it all work.

For me personally, managing all the calendars is the toughest part of any week, as I'm interfacing with eight people's schedules. I have to navigate my schedule (1), my two Parenting Partners' schedules (3), the older boys' schedules (5), the younger boys' schedules (7) and my wife's schedule (8). This balancing of schedules will sound familiar to anyone who is married or has been a part of a large family. No different and pretty routine.

Over these seventeen years it's actually been quite easy when someone needs to alter the usual schedule. The other party is usually flexible and obliges. "I have overtime at work on Tuesday, can you switch your pickup day?" or, "Hey, I have a business trip that came up suddenly, can you go to the birthday party this weekend?" "Sure, no problem." That's usually how smoothly it goes.

The children are also integrated casually when the adults pass along information through them. This happens in a number of ways. I'll say, "Hey Robert, please remind your mom that I have a business trip on Wednesday, and she needs to pick you up from school." I might say, "Hey Anthony, is your mom nearby? Can you remind her that you need to bring your swimsuit on Saturday?" This models responsibility for the boys. I may be chatting with Robert and Anna will pop into the picture and say, "Hey Frank, can you pick up Robert at 5:30 tomorrow instead of 6? I have to be somewhere." This models flexibility.

THANK GOODNESS FOR TECHNOLOGY

The mobile internet and apps have made Parenting Partnerships easier than ever. Video chat is indispensable. When the boys are with their mothers, we'll video chat almost every day, multiple times. I like to check in, ask about their day, and tell them I love them. When the boys are with me, their moms likewise video chat for the same reasons. Video chat has also strengthened the boys' relationships with extended family.

Text messaging is the Parenting Partner's number one way of communicating. Sometimes I text with Parenting Partners individually and we also have a three-person text thread with me, Anna, and Sophia. Another text thread features Natalie, myself and the two Parenting Partners. Now that Robert is sixteen and a half and has a phone we have some threads with him included as well. Direct dad-to-son texting is also an important tool. We've tried some more sophisticated family organizing apps like Cozi; which tracks appointments, school events, to-do lists, and more. It worked pretty well and there are plenty of similar apps to suit your needs. The net is that all of this would be much more difficult, if not impossible, in the pre-cell phone world without email, texting, online calendars and video chat.

IN-PERSON MEETINGS

Beyond all the digital tools at our disposal, we also have lengthy, in-person meetings a few times a year, if not more frequently, to set goals, discuss development milestones and plan large vacations. For example, we usually have a meeting in May to plan the entire summer vacation schedule. At first these meetings were just me and the Parenting Partners, then added Natalie, and a couple of years back Robert.

On a much more regular basis, when we Parenting Partners pick up our child, we exchange greetings, recap the past couple days, plans for the next twenty-four hours and then discuss the upcoming week. We talk about events or appointments that might require both parents to be in attendance, getting the boys together for some brother time, any outstanding "to do items", school or work related scheduling and lastly unusual changes to our routine, such as work travel. Special attention is paid to accomplishments or challenges we've experienced with the boys while in our care. The high-points are reiterated through text messages before and after.

There is another very valuable aspect to these in-person communications. The child gets to see their parents working together as a team, and in our case with the whole ecosystem, to prioritize the child's welfare. The level of communication, cooperation, respect and thoughtfulness that is extended in these meetings sets a great example and reinforces to the child that they are our number one priority.

Robert needs to hear the backstory, the possible options and the hoped for outcomes. We want to avoid presenting two different sides of a complex topic at different times and out of context. When appropriate, we want to provide him with an unfiltered view of how the plan formed. While these conversations go pretty well, they also involve a little bit of back and forth. We need to let him see how that plays out in a healthy way and witness different communication styles. We're teaching him how to be a respectful and communicative adult. Furthermore, now that he is sixteen we want / need to factor in his opinions and solidify his buy-in to the process, plan and outcomes.

Pro tip: everyone in the ecosystem should strive to over-communicate. The more communication the smoother everything goes. If there is any hesitancy to talk with each other, little details will slip through the cracks. The times when we have under-communicated have led to frustration and missed opportunities, in some cases impacting the child's activities. As Parenting Partners, we have to communicate even when it's uncomfortable or inconvenient because we have committed to prioritizing our child and providing them with the best opportunities possible.

THE AGE OF THE CHILD MATTERS

When the boys were really young, say birth to four-years-old, scheduling was much easier. This is because they are primarily home-based. They don't have extracurriculars, friends, hobbies, field trips, family outings, or birthday parties every weekend. In fact, when they're in the infant or toddler stage, many times you come to pick them up and they're napping. So, you end up sitting around and waiting. You should both be comfortable with spending time at one another's homes and with the other partner's caregivers and extended family.

Children aged five to ten are exploring their community. School is a constant with other events and activities added in. Anthony at different points has swim, soccer and basketball. This creates complexity in scheduling pick-ups and drop-offs at different venues at different times on different days. More communication and planning is needed. House pick-ups become easier as the kids usually come running out with their backpacks full of homework and dirty clothes.

Middle and early high school years are yet another dynamic, with Robert often setting his own activities and schedule and telling us when and where to pick him up after study sessions, student ambassador and clubs. As a high-schooler he started making a little money with gigs babysitting, baseball umpiring, and dog walking that further varied his schedule.

Through all of these phases, parenting requires constant, relaxed discussions with your child about the important topics that bring them joy and cause them stress. For Parenting Partners there are the added discussions to help normalize your child's unique origin story derived from their parent's decision to eschew marriage. We started these discussions early with each boy and nested the topic within a strong sentiment of love and devotion for our child and respect for one another. These conversations evolved yearly to match the child's emotional and intellectual growth and to address any societal interactions with kids or adults that caused them to be curious or unsure about our unique arrangement.

IS THERE EVER ENOUGH TIME

Robin Grille, author of *Heart-to-Heart Parenting* offers this insight in his article titled Parental Guilt: A Silent Epidemic, *"Parents everywhere agonize in secret: 'Where did I go wrong? Will my child be damaged because of what I did, or because of what I failed to do?' To make matters worse, these days there is so much more information out there about what babies and children need; we have doubled the fodder for self-recrimination."* [90] From my unique position as both a traditional parent and a Parenting Partner I can tell you that in both situations I feel the same pangs[91] of "parent guilt"[92] even though I constantly spend almost all of my free time with my four boys. I've never met a parent who feels 100% confident that they spent enough time with their kids or educated them to the utmost level. Every parent out there is just doing the best they can. They're trying to give their kid every advantage and provide them with every opportunity, regardless of their status. Also remember that, for many people, they would never even have children if not for a Parenting Partnership. So, the time away from your child in the structure of a Parenting Partnership is a small price to pay for the infinite joy you feel as a parent.

Overall, the day-to-day and week-to-week time management of a Parenting Partnership is the same as most parenting situations and is not as difficult as you might think. If you were in a traditional marriage, you would have to discuss daily details with your spouse. If you were divorced, you'd be coordinating with your ex. Parenting Partnerships are basically the same. It takes communication, flexibility, understanding, cooperation and organization. Anyone who has children can attest to this. Kids need love, guidance and attention no matter the situation and that takes a lot of time from both parents. Robert and Anthony have been given plenty of all three.

CONCLUSION

Modern society has gone through revolutionary changes over the past sixty years and this has had a disruptive effect on dating, marriage, conception and child-rearing. The megatrends that have caused this show no signs of reversing course. Parenting Partnerships are a logical and viable response to the baby-boomer led 80% failure rate of marriage and the difficulties that surround single parenthood. The benefits of Parenting Partnerships far outweigh the drawbacks. As traditional marriage continues to decline, millions of people who want to be parents will discover what we've learned through personal experience—that Parenting Partnerships are a healthy way to become a parent and have the child you've always dreamed of without the risks and downsides of single parenthood or a less-than-optimal marriage.

This book and similar stories provide concrete proof that Parenting Partnerships can produce extremely healthy outcomes for kids and parents. While my story of two Parenting Partnerships and a traditional marriage is an outlier, the learnings from my seventeen years of Parenting Partnerships show that it is a manageable and joyous situation that still allows for personal freedoms and the chance for true romantic love.

As you now understand, a Parenting Partnership is not something to be entered into lightly. It requires a great deal of thought, introspection, discussion, planning, and foresight. And that must happen *before* the partnership begins. If you follow the guidelines set forth in this book, you'll be well on your way to one of the most fulfilling aspects of life—raising a happy child in a loving environment.

A Parenting Partnership could very well be the first choice for many of you to have a child. For those in your twenties I'd still suggest another few years of being open to falling in love and getting into a Good | Great | Awesome Marriage. But the world being what it is, that traditional progression is simply not an option for millions of people. What I'm proposing is that, for the right person in the right life circumstance, Parenting Partnerships are superior to almost every other parenting option, and they can bring many wonderful blessings to your and your Parenting Partner's life. As with any arrangement between two people, not everything will go perfectly according to plan. There will likely be some short and long-term adversity in a Parenting Partnership, just as there is in any marriage, divorce, or single-parent household. But, the chances of having overall success are high and most of the decisions and work are front loaded with a lifetime of benefit on the backside.

The deepest wish when becoming parents is to shower your child with love, pass on all that you have learned, and enjoy watching your little one grow up. Parenting Partnership are pure and focused as these are the only reasons to enter into this form of parenting. There aren't any other unreasonable or unknown expectations—just fulfilling the dream of having a child you can love and guide toward adulthood.

HIGH PRAISE

As I write these final words, it has been seventeen and a half years since I accepted Anna's proposal to become a father through a Parenting Partnership and I have nothing but unequivocal praise for how this arrangement has impacted my life. My children are thriving, my partners and I are on excellent terms, and I've been able to marry a wonderful woman who not only accepts my life as it was, but was excited to expand our family in the traditional way.

Both of my Parenting Partners are deeply devoted mothers who love their sons as much as possible and have excelled as parents. Their lives and those of their immediate family are likewise much fuller in all ways.

Robert and Anthony are great kids who have bright futures and seem well developed to succeed in whatever they choose for their lives. They are also strongly bonded to one another and great big brother examples who we show off with pride to their two youngest brothers.

THE FUTURE OF PARENTING PARTNERSHIPS

Whether for you or for other people, we believe that Parenting Partnerships will become increasingly more common as it is a strong response to the present and future megatrends affecting the marriage and child dynamic.

Even as you finish this book, a Parenting Partnership may not be your first choice for your own future, but it should be on the radar and very near the top. I can't stress how important it is to make sure you choose the right person with whom to spend your life in marriage or as a Parenting Partner; don't let that be a frivolous or impulsive decision.

Always keep in mind that the happiest, healthiest children come from the happiest, healthiest homes. If your dream is to become a parent, you don't have to simply follow what society, culture, or family tell you is the "only right" way. Instead, consider what would create the best situation for you to be the best parent you can be. A mindful, mature, conscientious approach to a Parenting Partnership can be a wonderful life experience for you, your partner, your immediate and extended families, and your future child.

ACKNOWLEDGMENTS

My deepest thanks to my wife Natalie for our eleven-year life journey and five-year book journey. Thanks also to Chelsea, Chris, Mark, and Kelly and the hard working folks at NSS.

ENDNOTES

1 Schultz, Carrie S., "What Is The Difference Between Co-Parenting And Parallel Parenting?" Men's & Fathers' Rights Divorce Lawyers by Schultz & Associates, LLC, October 25, 2018, https://mensrightsdivorcelaw.com/blog/co-parenting-and-parallel-parenting/.

2 Pease Gadoua, Susan, "Why Choose a Parenting Marriage?" Psychology Today, March 29, 2017, https://www.psychologytoday.com/us/blog/contemplating-divorce/201703/why-choose-parenting-marriage.

3 Wang, Wendy & Taylor, Paul, "For Millennials, Parenthood Trumps Marriage," Pew Research Center, March 9, 2011, https://www.pewresearch.org/social-trends/2011/03/09/for-millennials-parenthood-trumps-marriage/.

4 Parker, Kim & Stapler, Renee, "As U.S. marriage rate hovers at 50%, education gap in marital status widens," Pew Research Center, September 14, 2017, https://www.pewresearch.org/fact-tank/2017/09/14/as-u-s-marriage-rate-hovers-at-50-education-gap-in-marital-status-widens/.

5 DePaulo, Bella, "A Half-Century of Fewer People Marrying: What Explains It?" Psychology Today, May 20, 2018, https://www.psychologytoday.com/ca/blog/living-single/201805/half-century-fewer-people-marrying-what-explains-it.

6 "Fertility rate, total (births per woman), The World Bank, https://data.worldbank.org/indicator/SP.DYN.TFRT.IN.

7   Johnson, Kenneth, "Deaths Exceeded Births in a Record Number of States in 2020," University of New Hampshire Carsey School of Public Policy, May 5, 2021, https://carsey.unh.edu/publication/snapshot/2020-deaths-exceeded-births-in-record-number-of-states.

8 Tavernise, Sabrina, "The U.S. Birthrate Has Dropped Again. The Pandemic May Be Accelerating the Decline," The New York Times, May 5, 2021, https://www.nytimes.com/2021/05/05/us/us-birthrate-falls-covid.html.

9 Morin, Amy, "How Parents Fighting Affects a Child's Mental Health," Verywell Family, November 11, 2019, https://www.verywellfamily.com/how-parents-fighting-affects-children-s-mental-health-4158375.

10 Wong, Brittany, "7 Ways You Can Damage Your Kids By Staying In A Bad Marriage," The Huffington Post, May 17, 2016, https://www.huffpost.com/entry/7-ways-you-can-damage-your-kids-by-staying-in-a-bad-marriage_n_573b4845e4b0646cbeeaf9a9.

11 "Marriages and Divorces," Centers for Disease Control and Prevention, Accessed June 21, 2022, https://www.cdc.gov/nchs/nvss/marriage-divorce.htm.

12 "32 Shocking Divorce Statistics," McKinley Irvin Family Law, October 30, 2012, https://www.mckinleyirvin.com/family-law-blog/2012/october/32-shocking-divorce-statistics/.

13 Steverman, Ben, "Millennials Are Causing the U.S. Divorce Rate to Plummet," Bloomberg, September 26, 2018, https://www.bloomberg.com/news/articles/2018-09-25/millennials-are-causing-the-u-s-divorce-rate-to-plummet.

14 Jeric, Nikolina, "15 Fascinating Sexless Marriage Statistics for 2022," 2Date4Love, January 20, 2021, https://2date4love.com/sexless-marriage-statistics/.

15 Pease Gadoua, Susan, "Why Choose a Parenting Marriage?" Psychology Today, March 29, 2017, https://www.psychologytoday.com/us/blog/contemplating-divorce/201703/why-choose-parenting-marriage.

16 Grover, Sean, "4 Reasons Why Bad Marriages are Worse for Kids Than Divorce," Relationship Resolution, July 4, 2017, https://relationshipresolution.com/articles/2017/7/4/4-reasons-why-bad-marriages-are-worse-for-kids-than-divorce.

17 Vitelli, Romeo, "Life After Divorce," Psychology Today, July 13, 2015, https://www.psychologytoday.com/us/blog/media-spotlight/201507/life-after-divorce

18 "Adverse Childhood Experiences (ACEs)," Centers for Disease Control and Prevention, Accessed June 21, 2022, https://www.cdc.gov/violenceprevention/aces/index.html.

19 Barcus, Jordan, "My divorce cost me $17,695 — these were the most surprising expenses I faced," Insider, January 1, 2020, https://www.businessinsider.com/cost-of-divorce-unexpected-surprising-expenses-2019-8.

20 Schneider, Daniel, "What Explains the Decline in First Marriage in the United States? Evidence from the Panel Study of Income Dynamics, 1969 to 2013," May 8, 2018, https://onlinelibrary.wiley.com/doi/10.1111/jomf.12481.

21 Wildsmith, Elizabeth, Manlove, Jennifer & Cook, Elizabeth, "Dramatic increase in the proportion of births outside of marriage in the United States from 1990 to 2016," Child Trends, August 8, 2018, https://www.childtrends.org/publications/dramatic-increase-in-percentage-of-births-outside-marriage-among-whites-hispanics-and-women-with-higher-education-levels.

22 https://www.singlemothersbychoice.org/

23 Clemons, Rick, "Facing A Mixed-Orientation Marriage With Gratitude And Hope," Huff Post, February 11, 2018, https://www.huffpost.com/entry/facing-a-mixed-orientation_b_14234452.

24 Brown, Anna, "Growing share of childless adults in U.S. don't expect to ever have children," Pew Research Center, November 19, 2021, https://www.pewresearch.org/fact-

tank/2021/11/19/growing-share-of-childless-adults-in-u-s-dont-expect-to-ever-have-children/.

25 Belkin, Douglas, "A Generation of American Men Give Up on College: 'I Just Feel Lost'," The Wall Street Journal, September 6, 2021, https://www.wsj.com/articles/college-university-fall-higher-education-men-women-enrollment-admissions-back-to-school-11630948233.

26 Tingley, Kim, "Why Are Sexually Transmitted Infections Surging?" The New York Times Magazine, May 17, 2022, https://www.nytimes.com/2022/05/17/magazine/sexually-transmitted-infections-surging.html.

27 Wolfinger, Nicholas, "Counterintuitive Trends in the Link Between Premarital Sex and Marital Stability," Institute for Family Studies, June 6, 2016, https://ifstudies.org/blog/counterintuitive-trends-in-the-link-between-premarital-sex-and-marital-stability.

28 O'Neill, Aaron, "Life expectancy (from birth) in the United States, from 1860 to 2020," Statista, June 21, 2022, https://www.statista.com/statistics/1040079/life-expectancy-united-states-all-time/.

29 Fisher, Richard, "Why teenagers aren't what they used to be," BBC, February 2, 2022, https://www.bbc.com/future/article/20220124-why-teens-arent-what-they-used-to-be.

30 Johnson, Stephen, "Why is 18 the age of adulthood if the brain can take 30 years to mature?" Big Think, January 31, 2022, https://bigthink.com/neuropsych/adult-brain/.

31 Painter, Kim, "As births decline in young women, they keep rising in 40-somethings. Here's why." USA Today, May 21, 2018, https://www.usatoday.com/story/news/2018/05/19/childbearing-why-women-40-s-having-more-babies/624028002/.

32 Tingley, Kim, "Why Are Sexually Transmitted Infections Surging?" The New York Times Magazine, May 17, 2022, https://www.nytimes.com/2022/05/17/magazine/sexually-transmitted-infections-surging.html.

33 Elkins, Kathleen, "Shark Tank's Kevin O'Leary says you should only get married if you plan to have kids," Insider, December 9, 2015, https://www.businessinsider.com/only-get-married-for-kids-2015-12?op=1.

34 "Why Women File 80 Percent of Divorces," DivorceSource.com, January 20, 2016, https://www.divorcesource.com/blog/why-women-file-80-percent-of-divorces/.

35 Perel, Esther, "Why Modern Love is So Damn Hard," Esther Perel, Accessed 22 January 2022, https://www.estherperel.com/blog/why-modern-love-is-so-damn-hard.

36 Howe, Edmund G, "Ethical issues when non-paternity is an incidental finding," MedCrave, January 21, 2021, https://medcraveonline.com/IPCB/ethical-issues-when-non-paternity-is-an-incidental-finding.html.

37 Barroso, Amanda, "More than half of Americans say marriage is important but not essential to leading a fulfilling

life," Pew Research Center, February 14, 2020, https://www.
pewresearch.org/fact-tank/2020/02/14/more-than-half-of-
americans-say-marriage-is-important-but-not-essential-to-
leading-a-fulfilling-life/.

38 Graf, Nikki, "Key findings on marriage and cohabitation
in the U.S.," Pew Research Center, November 6, 2019,
https://www.pewresearch.org/fact-tank/2019/11/06/key-
findings-on-marriage-and-cohabitation-in-the-u-s/.

39 Livingston, Gretchen, "Fewer than half of U.S. kids
today live in a 'traditional' family," Pew Research Center,
December 22, 2014, https://www.pewresearch.org/fact-
tank/2014/12/22/less-than-half-of-u-s-kids-today-live-in-a-
traditional-family/.

40 "Unmarried Childbearing," Centers for Disease Control
and Prevention, Accessed July 13, 2022, https://www.cdc.
gov/nchs/fastats/unmarried-childbearing.htm.

41 "Building Blocks for Father Involvement: Building Block
1--Appreciating How Fathers Give Children a Head Start,"
US Department of Health and Human Services, Head Start
Bureau, June 2004, https://eric.ed.gov/?id=ED543023.

42 "Maternal-Fetal Medicine," Cleveland Clinic, Accessed
July 12, 2022, https://my.clevelandclinic.org/florida/
departments/obgyn-womens-health/depts/obstetrics-and-
maternity-care/maternal-fetal-medicine#conditions-tab.

43 Rutgers University, "Older fathers put health of partners,
unborn children at risk: Men who delay fatherhood should

consult their doctor and consider banking sperm before age 35," ScienceDaily, May 13, 2019, www.sciencedaily.com/releases/2019/05/190513081409.htm.

44 Conrad, Marissa, "How Much Does IVF Cost?" Forbes Health, September 28, 2021, https://www.forbes.com/health/family/how-much-does-ivf-cost/.

45 "How Many Same-Sex Couples in the US are Raising Children?" Williams Institute, July 2018, https://williamsinstitute.law.ucla.edu/publications/same-sex-parents-us/.

46 Klein, Jessica, "The millennials choosing friends as sperm donors," BBC, February 2, 2022, https://www.bbc.com/worklife/article/20220128-the-millennials-choosing-friends-as-sperm-donors.

47 "Infertility," Centers for Disease Control & Prevention, Accessed July 6, 2022, https://www.cdc.gov/nchs/fastats/infertility.htm.

48 Leslie, Stephen et al., "Male Infertility," National Library of Medicine, February 14, 2022, https://pubmed.ncbi.nlm.nih.gov/32965929/.

49 "Natural family planning," Healthily, Accessed June 3, 2022, https://www.livehealthily.com/getting-pregnant/natural-family-planning.

50 Nguyen, Kara, "5 must-know facts about your fertility if you're trying to get pregnant," Shady Grove Fertility,

May 2022, https://www.shadygrovefertility.com/article/
must-know-facts-about-your-fertility-if-youre-trying-to-get-
pregnant/.

51 "Optimizing natural fertility: a committee opinion," The
American Society for Reproductive Medicine, January 2022,
https://www.asrm.org/globalassets/asrm/asrm-content/news-
and-publications/practice-guidelines/for-non-members/
optimizing_natural_fertility.pdf.

52 Shirazi, Talia, "Intrauterine insemination: IUI costs,
success rates, and factors that shape outcomes," Modern
Fertility, August 20, 2021, https://modernfertility.com/blog/
iui-costs-success-rates/.

53 Masters, Maria, "Using a Sperm Donor to Get
Pregnant," What to Expect, May 19, 2022, https://www.
whattoexpect.com/getting-pregnant/fertility-tests-and-
treatments/sperm-donor/.

54 Muthigi, Akhil et al,, "Clarifying the relationship
between total motile sperm counts and intrauterine
insemination pregnancy rates," Fertility and Sterility, June
6, 2021, https://www.sciencedirect.com/science/article/pii/
S0015028221000352?casa_token=EC1aS9rclVkAAAAA:F7
duph0V3UajWBXvrfhiSAaDMyMBNdw0IjowJHWOt-Jyfy
odtyJqM8UBo1m8xyRPgWn3LtR3hA#fig1.

55 Burke, Rennie et al., "How Do Individuals Who Were
Conceived Through the Use of Donor Technologies Feel
About the Nature of their Conception?" Center for Bioethics

Harvard Medical School, April 1, 2021, https://bioethics. hms.harvard.edu/journal/donor-technology.

56 Stöppler, Melissa Conrad, "In Vitro Fertilization (IVF) Process, Success Rates, Cost, and Effectiveness," EMedicine Health, Accessed June 1, 2022, https://www. emedicinehealth.com/in_vitro_fertilization/article_ em.htm#what_are_the_success_rates_for_ivf.

57 Conrad, Marissa, "How Much Does IVF Cost?" Forbes Health, September 28, 2021, https://www.forbes.com/ health/family/how-much-does-ivf-cost/.

58 "Surrogacy Pros & Cons: What You Should Know," Thompson Dove Law Group, LLC., Accessed June 3, 2022, https://tdlawgroup.com/home/surrogacy-and-assisted-reproduction/surrogacy-information/surrogacy-pros-cons/.

59 "West Coast Surrogacy Costs & Fees," West Coast Surrogacy Inc., Accessed June 3, 2022, https://www. westcoastsurrogacy.com/surrogate-program-for-intended-parents/surrogate-mother-cost.

60 "Types of Adoption," Adoption Center, Accessed June 3, 2022, https://adopt.org/types-adoptions.

61 "How Much Does It Cost To Adopt A Child?" American Adoptions, Accessed June 27, 2022, https://www. americanadoptions.com/adopt/why_does_private_adoption_ cost_so_much_money.

62 Granillo, Jason, "How Long Does it Take to Adopt a Child?" Adoption Network, Accessed January 31, 2022, https://adoptionnetwork.com/how-long-does-it-take-to-adopt-a-child/.

63 "Choosing a Closed Adoption: Pros and Cons to Consider," Texas Adoption Center, July 28, 2021, https://www.texasadoptioncenter.org/blog/closed-adoption-pros-and-cons/.

64 Linton, Deborah, "'I wanted to meet a mate and have a baby without wasting time': the rise of platonic co-parenting," The Guardian, October 31, 2020, https://www.theguardian.com/lifeandstyle/2020/oct/31/i-wanted-to-meet-a-mate-and-have-a-baby-without-wasting-time-the-rise-of-platonic-co-parenting.

65 "Ectopic pregnancy," Mayo Clinic, Accessed July 13, 2022, https://www.mayoclinic.org/diseases-conditions/ectopic-pregnancy/symptoms-causes/syc-20372088.

66 "Endometriosis," Mayo Clinic, Accessed July 12, 2022, https://www.mayoclinic.org/diseases-conditions/endometriosis/symptoms-causes/syc-20354656.

67 Jones, Lawrence R., "Platonic Parenting I: An Emerging Concept in an Ever-Changing World," New Jersey Law Journal, October 21, 2021, https://www.law.com/njlawjournal/2021/10/21/platonic-parenting-i-an-emerging-concept-in-an-ever-changing-world/?slretu rn=20220527185455.

68 Brown, Anna, "Growing share of childless adults in U.S. don't expect to ever have children," Pew Research Center, November 19, 2021, https://www.pewresearch.org/fact-tank/2021/11/19/growing-share-of-childless-adults-in-u-s-dont-expect-to-ever-have-children/.

69 Steinberg, Stacey, "Parent partnerships: A better way to co-parent," The Washington Post, March 8, 2016, https://www.washingtonpost.com/news/parenting/wp/2016/03/08/parent-partnerships-a-better-way-to-co-parent/.

70 "Child Custody and Support," Texas State Law Library, Accessed July 9, 2022, https://guides.sll.texas.gov/child-custody-and-support/child-custody.

71 Parker, Tim, "The Cost of Raising a Child in the United States," Investopedia, January 9, 2022, https://www.investopedia.com/articles/personal-finance/090415/cost-raising-child-america.asp.

72 Stefan, "Average Cost of Raising a Child," Balancing Everything, December 31, 2021, https://balancingeverything.com/average-cost-of-raising-a-child/.

73 "Types of Child Custody," FindLaw, Accessed July 12, 2022, https://www.findlaw.com/family/child-custody/types-of-child-custody.html.

74 "How Much Does it Cost to Give Birth if I Don't Have Health Insurance?" True Coverage, July 4, 2022, https://truecoverage.com/how-much-does-it-cost-to-give-birth/.

75 Berger, Chloe, "Insurance is hiding how expensive it is to have a kid: Nearly $20,000 for every baby born in the U.S." Fortune Magazine, July 13, 2022, https://finance.yahoo.com/news/insurance-hiding-expensive-kid-nearly-185829423.html.

76 Traverso, Vittoria and Robbins, Jake, "Is 'platonic parenting' the relationship of the future?" BBC, December 19, 2018, https://www.bbc.com/worklife/article/20181218-is-platonic-parenting-the-relationship-of-the-future.

77 Nigro, Carmen, "Names Have Meaning: A Research Guide for Baby Names and Family Names," New York Public Library, June 1, 2015, https://www.nypl.org/blog/2015/06/01/names-research-guide.

78 Jarrett, Christian, "How your name affects your personality," BBC, May 26, 2021, https://www.bbc.com/future/article/20210525-how-your-name-affects-your-personality.

79 Ben-Joseph, Elana Pearl, "Bonding With Your Baby," Nemours Kids Health, Accessed July 10, 2022, https://kidshealth.org/en/parents/bonding.html.

80 "Hysterosalpingogram (HSG)," Women's Health Care, Accessed June 1, 2022, https://www.womenshealthcarewaukesha.com/gyn/hysterosalpingogram.

81 Pells, Racheal, "Genetic Screening Now Lets Parents Pick the Healthiest Embryos," Wired, July 5, 2022, https://www.wired.com/story/genetic-screening-ivf-healthiest-embryos/.

82 Neuman, Kenley, "Preconception Genetic Testing 101: A Complete Guide," Virginia Physicians For Women, Accessed June 3, 2022, https://vpfw.com/blog/preconception-genetic-testing-101-a-complete-guide/.

83 "STDs during Pregnancy – CDC Basic Fact Sheet," Centers for Disease Control and Prevention, Accessed June 3, 2022, https://www.cdc.gov/std/pregnancy/stdfact-pregnancy.htm.

84 Hanson, Lauren, "Premarital counseling can decrease divorce rates, psychologist says," The Daily Universe, July 6, 2017, https://universe.byu.edu/2017/07/06/premarital-counseling-can-decrease-divorce-rates-psychologist-says/.

85 Bannow, Tara, "Local company creates Klingon dictionary," The Minnesota Daily, November 17, 2009, https://mndaily.com/186847/uncategorized/local-company-creates-klingon-dictionary/.

86 "Management of Ruptured Ovarian Cyst," John Hopkins Medicine, Accessed July 12, 2022, https://www.hopkinsmedicine.org/health/treatment-tests-and-therapies/management-of-ruptured-ovarian-cyst?amp=true.

87 "PCOS (Polycystic Ovary Syndrome) and Diabetes," Centers for Disease Control and Prevention, Accessed July 12, 2022, https://www.cdc.gov/diabetes/basics/pcos.html.

88 Dugas, Carla and Slane, Valori, "Miscarriage," National Library of Medicine, Accessed June 4, 2022, https://www.ncbi.nlm.nih.gov/books/NBK532992/.

89 Gurevich, Rachel, "When the Clinical Signs of Pregnancy Occur," Very Well Family, April 20, 2020, https://www.verywellfamily.com/clinical-pregnancy-1960106.

90 Grille, Robin, "Parent Guilt: A Silent Epidemic," The Natural Child Project, Accessed July 16, 2022, https://www.naturalchild.org/articles/robin_grille/parent_guilt.html.

91 Jacobson, Sheri, "Dad Guilt? When "Bad Dad" Worries Bring You Down," Harley Therapy, April 29, 2021, https://www.harleytherapy.co.uk/counselling/dad-guilt.htm

92 Brody, Lauren Smith, "Why mom guilt is the biggest lie of all," Today's Parent, March 5, 2021, https://www.todaysparent.com/family/parenting/why-mom-guilt-is-the-biggest-lie-of-all/.

CPSIA information can be obtained
at www.ICGtesting.com
Printed in the USA
LVHW101554280423
745516LV00001B/24